NINE GA'
THE KINGDOM OF SHADOWS

LOST BOOKS OF THE NECRONOMICON
(AMETHYST EDITION)

Edited by Joshua Free

*Nostalgia Edition of the Mardukite Year-1 "Liber-9" materials
"The Unpublished Conclusion to the Necronomicon"
published in 2009 by Mardukite Truth Seeker Press and
reprinted in the Necronomicon Anunnaki Bible Year-1 anthology*

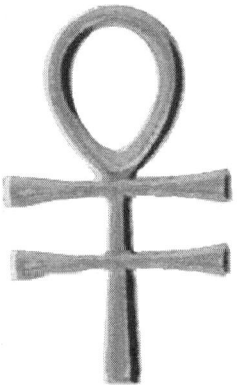

© 2012, Joshua Free

No part of this publication may be reproduced in any form or by any means, electronic or mechanical, including photocopying, recording, or by any information storage or retrieval system, without permission in writing from the publisher.

Other Related Titles By Joshua Free

Necronomicon Anunnaki Bible
(Liber N, L, G & 9)

Sumerian Religion (Liber 50)
Babylonian Myth & Magic (Liber 51)
Necronomicon Revelations (Liber R)

Gates of the Necronomiconm
(Liber 50, 51 & R)

Book of Marduk by Nabu (Liber W)

Mardukite Wizards of the Wastelands (WoW)

Magan Magic -or- *Necronomicon Spellbook I (Liber E)*
Maqlu Magic -or- *Necronomicon Spellbook II (Liber M)*
Beyond the Ishtar Gate -or- *Necro. Spell. III (Liber C)*

Mesopotamian Magic -or- *Necronomicon Workbook*
(Liber E, M & C)

Nabu Speaks! (Liber 12)
Enochian Magic & The Kabbalah (Liber K)
Necro. for Beginners -or- *Stargate to the Abyss (Liber 555)*

History of the Necronomicon
(Liber K, 555 & 12)

Arcanum (Liber A)

Book of Elven-Faerie (Liber D)
Draconomicon (D2)
Druidry (D3)

A Complete Course Curr. In Druidry -or- *The Druid Compleat*
(D1, D2 & D3)

The 2012 Mardukite Core Nostalgia Editions
by Joshua Free

NECRONOMICON : The Babylonian Grimoire (Lapis Edition)
NECRONOMICON LITURGY & LORE (Ruby Edition)
NECRONOMICON GATEKEEPERS GRIMOIRE (Emerald Edition)
NINE GATES OF THE KINGDOM OF SHADOWS (Amethyst Edition)

Between the idea and the reality
Between the motion and the act
Falls the Shadow

Between the conception and creation
Between emotion and the response
Falls the Shadow

Between the desire and the spasm
Between the potency and the existence
Between the essence and the descent. . .

Falls the Shadow

– T.S. Eliot

Book Design & Layout by Joshua Free

The contents of this book were first pubished in 2009
as part of an esoteric occult underground serial.

For the complete cycle of this current book,
please refer to the Year-1 composite Liber-N+L+G+9 anthology
Necronomicon Anunnaki Bible by Joshua Free
now available in the revised and espanded 2012 Fifth Edition.

NINE GATES OF THE KINGDOM OF SHADOWS

LOST BOOKS OF THE NECRONOMICON
(AMETHYST EDITION)

Edited by Joshua Free

*Nostalgia Edition of the Mardukite Year-1 "Liber-9" materials
"The Unpublished Conclusion to the Necronomicon"
published in 2009 by Mardukite Truth Seeker Press and
reprinted in the Necronomicon Anunnaki Bible Year-1 anthology*

**MARDUKITE
CHAMBERLAINS**

TABLE OF CONTENTS

Preface to the 2012 Nostalgia Editions 11

Novem Portis – Nine Gates 15

The Delomelanicon 21

Tablet-H Series:
   The Book of Headaches & Demonologie 27

Tablet-J Series:
   The Book of Al-Jilwah & Melek Ta'us 55

Tablet-Q Series:
   The Book of Qlippoth & Other Side 71

Tablet-I Series:
   The Tablets of Inform & Cypher Manuscript 85

**MARDUKITE
CHAMBERLAINS**

PREFACE TO THE 2012 NOSTALGIA EDITIONS

"More than simply a book imagined by a fantasy horror writer, or the product of some intensive Mesopotamian investigations in the 1970's, the NECRONOMICON is a piece of human consciousness, a primordial archetype that has existed in the backwaters of the mind for thousands of years. During a "new age" of revivals in ancient paganism and earth oriented spirituality, people have flocked to the ranks of neo-paganism, Wicca, Druidry and Scientology, and for good reason: the state of the world is in demand for a complete shift in human awareness. And while H.P. Lovecraft may have been alluding to such a tradition nearly one hundred years ago (even if only subconsciously) and the 1960's witnessed a gigantic practical rebirth in such traditions, it was really in the late 1970's that a separate but synchronous mainstream awakening occurred: the renewed interest in the the most antiquated Sumerian and Babylonian mysteries, specifically the role of the ANUNNAKI, Great Gods who once roamed the Earth and became the figures of our ancient mythologies..."*

The Mardukite Research Organization was founded on the Summer Solstice in 2008 during the underground release of "*Arcanum*" by Joshua Free. At its inception, the group was extraordinarily small but pointedly grew exponentially as soon as it began to make an online internet presence.

In 2009, the Mardukite Chamberlains began releasing their underground publications as part of an extraordinarily extensive version of what many people's debut into the realm of Mesopotamian esoterica had been – the Necronomicon.

---

* The initial lines introducing the "*Necronomicon: The Babylonian Grimoire*" Nostalgic 2012 'Lapis Edition' by Joshua Free.

The original versions of the 2009 'Mardukite Core' were all elaborately designed limited edition handcrafted tomes that later only appeared in the consolidated anthology titled 'Necronomicon Anunnaki Bible'. It consisted of the 'Necronomicon (of Joshua Free)' (Liber-N) in June of 2009 and three subsequent titles, 'Necronomicon Liturgy & Lore' (Liber-L), the 'Necronomicon Gatekeeper's Grimoire' (Liber-G) and the 'Nine Gates of the Kingdom of Shadows' or 'Necronomicon Shadows' (Liber-9).

Although the entire 'Year-1' anthology has been available exclusively as the 'Necronomicon Anunnaki Bible' for over four years, the 'Mardukite Truth Seeker Press' has decided to release a 'nostalgia edition' in 2012 of the original 'Mardukite Core' for those who are new to the mysteries and to rekindle the original flavor of the mystique that was ascertained by those involved with the early development of the materials.

In early 2012 a condensed, compact and abridged edition of the 'Necronomicon Anunnaki Bible' appeared on the scene as a reissue of the original 'lapis edition'. To coincide with this effort, a similarly designed reissue of the remaining 2009 'gem series' (as it was called then) is intended for release.

Following popular demand, the previously released 2012 'Lapis Edition' Necronomicon actually included more material than simply 'Liber-N' and thus differed from the original edition, these companions: 'Liber L', 'Liber G' and 'Liber-9', were all designed to match the original format and content as much as possible given the preexisting difference in production style. We hope you enjoy.

~Joshua Free
31, October 2012,
Mardukite West Coast Satellite Offices of California

NINE GATES OF THE KINGDOM OF SHADOWS

LOST BOOKS OF THE NECRONOMICON
(AMETHYST EDITION)

Edited by Joshua Free

*Nostalgia Edition of the Mardukite Year-1 "Liber-9" materials
"The Unpublished Conclusion to the Necronomicon"
published in 2009 by Mardukite Truth Seeker Press and
reprinted in the Necronomicon Anunnaki Bible Year-1 anthology*

NOVEM PORTIS – NINE GATES*

The path of the Mystery Tradition has, up until now, led the seeker along a vast array of "lights" and "images" - a "Ladder of Lights" (as it were) – tracing the phantasmal images of the material world back to their Source. But it is not the glamorous procurement of further persona and personality upgrades that the seeker is after, rather it is the absolution of the same, those which have already been acquired and are but weights to keep you bound to the material world.

So the seeker passes the Gates of Life seeking to bring the parts of the whole together – if they be so lucky. Too often it is the separation of the whole into more esoteric parts that merely ends with further separating the person from the Source.

The emphasis should not be on the bedazzlement attainable to the psyche of this world to delight in making some gematric or symbolic link – when all is actually connected in equality and oneness – not just to be found in one or two "sacred" relationships between attributes and forces. This is never fully realized in the World of Light that we become accustomed to because it exists already in a state of separation from the World of Darkness. Polarity. The point is not necessarily the glorification of the Darkness either. Just

---
* Excerpted from the *Liber-R* edition ("*Necronomicon Revelations*"), though it first appeared in the 2009 Amethyst Edition of *Liber-9* – initially released as "*Nine Gates of the Kingdom of Shadows: The Unpublished Conclusion to the Necronomicon of Joshua Free.*" Originally untitled, *Liber-9* was also known to the Mardukite Chamberlains as '*Necronomicon Shadows.*'

as many people succumb to the trappings of the Darkness as they do the Light and both are existing in a duality that is contrary to the Oneness that is the Source. Duality is not Oneness.

So, what does one do?

You can climb the Ladder of Lights and thereby unify the manifold natures of the existences found in the Light – but is this the end?

* * * * * * *

Working back up the Tree of Life‡, the seeker has uncovered a very dangerous glitch in the system... this is not all there is. But where is it?

And how is it that we can confront this hidden aspect for wholeness?

How do we get to the other side?

After having traversed the Gates of this Universe using the secrets of Babylon, the seeker inevitably moves passed the

---

‡ *Tree of Life* – a specific reference to the '*kabbalah*', a Semitic (Judeo) metaphysical model adopted from the earlier Assyrian and Sumerian '*Tree of Life*' modelled in the 'stargate formulae' or 'Babylon codex' as displayed in the lore of *Liber-G*, the *Necronomicon Gatekeepers Grimoire (2012 Nostalgic Emerald Edition)*, the 2012 *Book of Gates* full-color ceremonial edition and, as goes without saying, the complete Mardukite Year-1 *Liber-N+L+G+9* anthology '*Necronomicon Anunnaki Bible*'. See also *Liber-K* ('*Enochian Magic & The Kabbalah*' or in the Year-4 *Liber-K+555+12* anthology '*History of the Necronomicon*') or '*The Truth Seeker's Guide to the Kabbalah*' edited by Joshua Free.

final doorway and is able to glean a look behind the curtain... and there is nothing more horrifying than what one will find. All we have done and worked towards, all we have quested for in our endeavors into the Light and into the System and when the curtain is peeled back it is only to reveal – Nothingness... *the Primordial Abyss.*

All of the systems in the mind that have given form their meaning has washed away and the realization of the illusion is paralyzing. For when we had our "Wizard of Oz" to toy with in our minds, we could at the very least laugh in our own folly at being fooled in the game of some supernatural crazed madman behind the curtains. At the very least things could be made to make sense – *systematically.* But now at the cusp of reality and sanity, we know better...

Before you is the Other Side of the Tree... Crossing the Abyss... Into the Beyond... You have reached the edge. You are have reached – *the Shadows.*

* * * * * * *

After the rise of the Hermetic Order of the Golden Dawn in the late 1800's (and perhaps also such groups as the Theosophical Society) the metaphysical world of the mystics would seem to have begin appearing in the public spotlight, or at the very least carry an illusion of being maintained in public view. With this followed the widespread use of medieval grimoires – many of them somehow involved with figures like MacGregor Mathers and Aleister Crowley. Organizations relating to these individuals, such as the GD, OTO (Ordo Templi Orientis) and the lesser known AA (Argentium Astrum) begin to influence mystical practices and underground traditions among the multitudes on the surface world.

While we are naturally concerned with the subject of the Mardukite (Egypto-Babylonian and Sumerian) *Necronomicon* and its relationship to the Great Mysteries, the association of modern pseudoepigrapha (literally *artifical writings*) is not limited to even a book called the "*Necronomicon*" - for such is just a name, as is "*Al Azif*" - or anything else we want to definitively give a solid form too – that which cannot be solidified – that which has not meant to be solidified.

THE DELOMELANICON

"*El Club Dumas*" was released in Spain in 1993. The American English-speaking audience would have to wait three years to find "*The Club Dumas*" on their shelves. Arturo Perez-Reverte's masterpiece doomed to be lost amidst the mysteries of Agatha Christie and Sue Grafton. The main character of the novel, set in a dusty environment of Antiquarian book-selling, is on a quest to uncover the truth of a lost fragment or chapter of the serial by Alexander Dumas, the famous "Three Musketeers". While doing so, Corso is culled into a different kind of quest... and there are surprisingly more people aware of this influence of this modern tale then you might originally suspect – as it is also known by another name. The name:

Nine Gates of the Kingdom of Shadows.

Curiously, the work has thus far escaped the inevitability of occult pseudoepigrapha – from its Spanish edition we deduce "*Nine Doors to the Kingdom of Darkness*," though the American audience prefers the semantics of "*Gates*" to "portals" and thus too, the "*Shadows*" to the "Darkness". The American audiences are also more receptive to video media then literary and thus was probably the inclination Roman Polanski carried with him in filming "*The Ninth Gate*" with Johnny Depp [Relesed via Lions-Gate in 1999 and now Artisan DVD and Blu-ray]. Depp's performance is astounding as always – and the wood-carved engravings shown so often in the film are actually taken from those found in Reverte's novel.

It would surprise many occultists to note that the vein of pseudo-epigrapha runs deep within the mystic stream – reaching all too familiar works as the *"Keys of Solomon"* or even the *"Book of Abramelin"* – it comes by no surprise that we should see the rise within this age of more tales of such "books within books" - "fantasies about fantasies" - for we have undoubtedly reached our ends in the world of Light and must by necessity reach out to the Shadows.

Assuming the lore of the *Nine Gates*, let us say that the work is based on yet too another book – furthering our psyche down the literary rabbit hole. The *"Delomelanicon"* (which is unarguably another vision of the *Necronomicon* Cycle) is a book reported to have been written by the "Devil himself" as a guide to "his followers." The work, said to have once been in the possession of King Solomon, reaches the realm of Medieval Sorcery in 1666 by Aristide Torchia, who publishes his "version" of the "Devil's Notebook" as *"De Umbrarum Regni Novem Portis."*

Both Torchia and all but three copies of this work are burned by the Church. The title, *"Delomelanicon,"* the current editor transliterates to mean *"Book of Summoning the Darkness"* (very similar to the coveted but equally fantasy-based witches *Book of Shadows*) -- although some Chamberlains have preferred the translation *"Invocation of Darkness"* [as given in the Soto translation of *El Club Dumas*].

If we lend a thought to this for a moment, leaving the trappings of semantic vocabulary and verification of medieval sorcerer's grimoires aside – consider a book then that has been given to a class of followers of an entity contrary to the accepted "God On Duty" – considered a devil to one side and a savior to the other. Immediately, when thinking of the politics that arose in ancient Mesopotamia, beings like

Marduk and Enki are immediately conjured to mind – or some specific alien intelligence that might have reason for leading folks back through the Gates. And if they would indeed be hidden in the folds "between" the Realm or Reality of Light we see everyday, then they would most certainly belong to the Shadows – *and the spaces between spaces.*

The archetype conjured to mind by the "*Nine Gates*" is very similar to the *Necronomicon*. There is, at the very least, an obvious emphasis on the symbolism of "portals", "thresholds" and "gateways" – such as is inseparably paramount to this lore. Following the esoteric and occult traditions, the "Gates" are introduced to the Seeker under the guise of "Darkness," because such was (and remains to be) the perception of what is "forbidden" and "hidden" knowledge – at least from the perspective of the Relam of Light. For, even as Peter Levenda has said so concisely of the "Simonian" *Necronomicon*: "It is a book about Darkness."§ Levenda reiterates that it is NOT a book about "pacts with devils" or anything so trivial and trite as you might see with the *Grand Grimoire* (*Red Dragon*), etc. – but more importantly it is an ancient, nearly prehistoric methodology for *understanding the Darkness.*

Roman Polanski, as we can see by his choice of directing the "*Ninth Gate*" movie, is interested in the esoteric enigma of the *Necronomicon* – and what is interesting is that as a result, both Kenneth Grant and "Simon" have acknowledged (in their works) the contribution as some-thing of a personal nature. Not even knowing this, one can easily compare the "*Ninth Gate*" movie to "*El Club Dumas*" and inst-

---

§ Quoted from the PlusUltra podcast produced by Tracy Twyman. Peter Levenda is widely reputed to be the primary spokesperson for the Simon *Necronomicon*.

instantly recognize where the emphasis lies. Simon, in his book "*Dead Names*" explains that:

> "Anyone who met me in those days in the 1970's would recognize the Johnny Depp character: glasses, beard, black clothes, black raincoat, bag over one shoulder. The intrigue that follows some of the events in the real story [of the publication of the Simonian *Necronomicon*] including the references to wealthy individuals who sought the power of the book for themselves."

Those familiar with the "*other side*" of the Mystery Tradition are probably aware of the O.T.O. series of trilogies produced by Kenneth Grant. The final volume of this sequence of literature is called "*The Ninth Arch*" and it was released in 2002 – three years after the "*Ninth Gate*" movie was released (and almost a decade after the birth of "*El Club Dumas*"). The current editor's opinion is only that the title bore some synchronicity with the other. In this case however, the designation of "Arch" has a dual meaning, both to the idea of a "Gateway" but also the semantic and quasi-linguistic parallels (something Grant is essentially obsessed with) between "Arch" and "Arachnid" [note: ARaCHnid].

So now, thanks to Grant, we have the Spider to add to the equation – for the Book of the Spider or "*Grimoire of the Spider*" is given there, the "*Grimoire of the Night*" – that is on the "other side of the tree" once the initiate has worked through the "*Grimoire of the Light.*" The Spider transmissions are known in the O.T.O. as both "Book 29" and "OKBISh" (a word that Grant states is related to the word "Spider" form a Mesopotamian root).

All of this suggests that beneath the surface of the light, and in the *"betweens,"* there is as yet another part to the mystery of the seeker – the "Darkness" – "The Shadows." In most casts, the Seeker will just rush to throw light against the screen again, impressing images from their own experiences in the light – not allowing the self-honest experience to unfold.

We need not materialize demonic images or cast fears before us only to allow them to become manifest by our own will – as such is not the true nature of the Shadows. Such falseness has only been created within the fragmented and fractured minds of men who further the necessity for the Shadows as they cling to the Light.

For what greater horror could man behold in the Realm of Light, then to reach the unspeakable realization that is most capable of shattering their delicate human psyche (and perhaps the dissolution of the Ego) – that it is no demon or gruesome vision to behold – but the full experience that the material world is a mere veil to something else. It is not the ends in itself, only but a *means*.

But how can reality come apart at the seams?

For, we are a nation of civilized and enlightened men are we not?

Surely even humans have come to take the gear-grinding world for granted and the systems and boundaries that keep things in "check" are also in fear of dissolution – including monetary and political – as even George Hay notes, in his Preface to the *R'lyeh Text*, concerning the world changes that have appeared on the planet since the *Necronomicon* cycle revival in the 1970's noticing:

> "... the dissolution of 'fixed' and 'given' groupings of Nation-States, and, far more important, of the belief systems that had until recently been holding them together."

Considering that the Lightworkers have further taken their fragmented human psyche and placed greater limits and sanctions of "good" and "evil" on all existence, the perpetuation of the duality continues unresolved in the universe.

By casual interpretation of Mardukite *Necronomicon* lore – on might say that mankind was in actuality separated from the Source to exist in a polarized world. But humans also further this separation from the Source over the course of their lives by lengthening the distance between perceived opposites instead of seeking harmony – *a return to the Source*. So long as the separation is maintained in the mind, manifestations of fear, jealousy, discord and the like will continue to be given existence in "reality" and confirmed by the psyche.

NINE GATES OF THE KINGDOM OF SHADOWS

LOST BOOKS OF THE NECRONOMICON
(AMETHYST EDITION)

Edited by Joshua Free

*Nostalgia Edition of the Mardukite Year-1 "Liber-9" materials
"The Unpublished Conclusion to the Necronomicon"
published in 2009 by Mardukite Truth Seeker Press and
reprinted in the Necronomicon Anunnaki Bible Year-1 anthology*

– Mardukite "Liber-9" Amethyst Tablet Collection –

THE BOOK OF HEADACHES

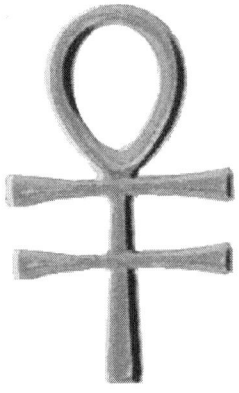

Tablet-H Series

– Mardukite "Liber-9" Amethyst Tablet Collection –

**MARDUKITE
CHAMBERLAINS**

THE BOOK OF HEADACHES & THE DEMONOLOGIE

The ancient world would appear, at first glance, to be composed of little else but fictitious "evil spirits" and the superstitious fools that fuel them with belief. To take the naïve historian's or mythographer's perspective might be convenient to some – but to a Seeker of the True Words, we cannot succumb to such surface interpretations.

The infamous Maklu "Burning" Tablets[1] have already made an appear-ance once in modern times – though they have not been given the full attention as yet that they deserve – but the Seeker may be less aware of other tablet series from similar origins, mainly:

> *Surpu Tablets* ("Consuming Demons")
> *Utukku Limnuti Tablet Series* ("Book of Evil Spirits")
> *Ti'i Tii* ("Book of Headaches")
> *Asakki Marsuti* ("Fevers & Sickness")
> *Labarto* ("The Hag-Demon")
> *Nis Kati* ("Raising [Lifting] of the Hand")[2]

In the Babylonian system, the priesthood dedicated to the exorcisms and banishment of ill-fortune (thought to be br-

---

1 See the *"M-Series"* Tablets from *Liber-N* in the Lapis Edition *'Necronomicon* or within the complete Mardukite Year-1 *Liber-N+L+G+9* anthology, *Necronomicon Anunnaki Bible* – with complete translation from *Liber-M ('Maqlu Magic'* or *'Necronomicon Spellbook II')* in the revised and expanded fifth edition of the *Bible*.
2 *Nis Kati* tablet series has served significant in the *Mardukite Research Organization* in regard to devotional prayers and incantation stylings of Babylonian priestly or religious magic.

ought on by the people's thoughts and deeds themselves, or those of another – e.g. wicked sorcerer) are called the "*asipu*" or "*masmasu*."[3] While it has been thought that all forms of "witchcraft" and "sorcery" (essentially "magic") were deemed evil, this is not remotely the case. In addition to the obviously mystical nature of the priesthood, these "wizards" and "witch-doctors" were actually given a highly esteemed class-status of combating against the "evil" sorcery cast by the lower class "hostile" and "wicked" ones.[4]

The "Words of Power" associated with both the subtle conjuring of the "daemons" or the violent exorcisms of the "evil genius" - whether it be by the most holy Roman Catholic Ritulae or the most diabolic of grimoires (e.g. the "Grand Grimoire" and "Dragon" grimiores – which occupy the same mythological paradigm as Catholicism and Judaism) are always of the "highest" - or else to say: "Holy Names" (e.g. Tetragrammaton). This is because the vibrations of the Material World occupy under the governance of the Material Ruler or Lord of the Earth,[5] which may have appeared in the past as a "Source God" but of which is only a "cyclic god". Exceptions within this system are the co-creators of this system, which is not Absolute, but a separation or shadow from the whole.

It has always been the "Supernal Trinities" and "Unspeakable Names" that carries both the avenging hunter and the glorifying worshiper of the "daemon" shadow; and the wise

---

3 Pronounced *mash-mashu*.
4 There is a distinction made between the magic of the 'realm', practiced by the priests in the temple for the benefit of the kingdom ('realm') and the magic used outside of the 'realm' by those who are not initiated and who use the powers self-servingly.
5 *Lord of the Earth* – literally "ENKI" in Mesopotamia; EN = lord (or high priest), KI = earth.

appear to use the systematic hierarchy of the "highest" to achieve these ends. For in the ancient times we see the priests of Eridu and Babylon calling to Marduk to appeal to his farther Enki. By the time of the Jewish mystics, such as we find in the "Book of Abramelin", this title has been generalized to Adonai, meaning simply, Lord of the Earth, though fundamentalist monotheists can only perceive the notion as "God – Source." Catholic priests and Christian sciences have adopted the name of "Jesus" as Adonai for the Piscean Age, something that many occultists actually find logical.

No different then we find among the cornucopia of anecdotal paranormal experiences today, the ancients had their run-ins with what contemporary society once generalized as "ghosts" - meaning the ethereal spiritual presence of an ancestral ("dead") spirit, or rather an spirit that returns due to its "unrest" or difficulty in "crossing". These are called "*edimmu*" ("E.DI.IM.MI") in Babylonian (Assyrian) lexicons. Another is called the "*utukku.*"

Although later interpreted to be a "daemon" (without being distinguished for its beneficent nature), the "*lamassu*" is a "positive" guardian spirit that is called forth in many of the tablet rites. It is hard to separate, in all cases, the difference between this spirit and the "*sedu*" guardian, but the combined lore of these led to the later Assyrian belief in "guardian angels" that was carried over into the Judeo-Christian beliefs until present times.

Essential to the craft of the priest is an adherence to the elements of the Material World in their material workings, however spiritual. Given that the function of the "healer" also fell upon the temple-priests, the tablets show evidence for a practice of spiritual medicine coupled with natural cures, lore of such has been revived in contemporary medicine. The appearance of the "elements of life", both physically and figuratively, appear in the ritual observances, specifically the "waters of life" and the "fires of life" which are considered purifying and cleansing, but also deceptively destructive. The "blood of life" and "breath of life" is added via the enactment of the ceremony to its ends.

Concerning the "bans" or "tabu" ("taboo") of the ancient tradition – many of them are actually placed on statures of healthy and sanitary living. For example, the more obvious including the body of a corpse... or of a woman who is menstruating... or the body of a young maiden girl... it is these social restrictions, taboos or "bans" that are placed on "civilized" man as a means of preserving order above that which might be found in the animal kingdom, which can be found to have far fewer of such boundaries.

Alleged "mind daemons" appear to await us around every corner seeking to thwart the hearts and actions of men away from the adherence to such. Whatever the nature, when someone goes "against the grain" bringing chaos into a given system, repercussions (even in the form of "thought-formed daemons") emerge.

The role of "sympathetic magic" in these affects cannot be overlooked. Given the vivid descriptions we have been given to draw off from ancient tablets, we see evidence for the stereotypical "voodoo-doll" as perhaps the most ancient recorded "folk charm" - used to represent a psychic target for either side as they essentially may be used to curse or remove curses or heal.

Representative figures made of wax frequently appear. In fact the Book of Burnings & the Maklu[6] can even be seen as a literal interpretation of the burning, melting, waxen images: "Ceremonial burnings in metaphoric effigy are usually performed with waxen dolls "made in the image of your enemy." Elsewhere it explains that "a waxen doll may be cursed over a flame and then melted into a cauldron".

The idea of connecting to the spirit or "soul" of a being via some waxen or natural-made image can be connected to the mystical practices of the Babylonians, Egyptians and Semitic tribes.

There are significant "sympathetic" powers attained via the knowledge and use of one's name – which is also to say the "true-name" - of a spirit or entity (embodied or not). As *R.C. Thompson* writes (paraphrasing *Lejean*): "The modern Abyssinian believes in demons being constantly on the watch to steal a Christian's name if they can, and it is the custom to conceal the real name by which a person is baptized with."

The Egyptian grimoire translated by Budge offers a rite by which aspects of the powers described are combined in combating the daemon "APEP" - a waxen figure is made in his image along with the name being written thereupon. The charm is burned to "bind" the spirit [the text reads: "destroy"; such seems unlikely by a single magician against this archetypal chaos in the Egyptian pantheon].

---

6 See the "*M-Series*" Tablets from *Liber-N* in the Lapis Edition '*Necronomicon* or within the complete Mardukite Year-1 *Liber-N+L+G+9* anthology, *Necronomicon Anunnaki Bible* – with complete translation from *Liber-M ('Maqlu Magic*' or '*Necronomicon Spellbook II*') in the revised and expanded fifth edition of the *Bible*.

The concept of cleanliness with sanity can be traced back to the roots of the word in Indo-European history, and to emphasize further the point, the ideas of uncleanliness, sin and demons are all synonymous among the ancients. The violation of health taboos also contributed to the connection between cleanliness and sin – though prior to these learned behaviors, the origins may have a much more ceremonial inclination – as described in Morgenstern's *Doctrine of Sin in the Babylonian Religion* –

> "the expressions: sin, uncleanliness, sickness, possession by evil spirits, are pure synonyms. They denote an evil state of the body, the result of the divine anger... sin must have been originally purely ritual. Either the man had neglected to offer his sacrifice, or else had not offered it properly."

It is important to note that before the sacrifices could be offered properly, a person would have first needed a "ritual cleansing" - furthering again the combined significance.

ANUNNAKI MANDALA OF PROTECTION

<u>Description</u> – To be said in the magick circle by the priest who has fashioned seven winged figures placed before him.

<u>Directions for the practitioner</u>:
  To spread a dark garment on their "upraised arms."
  To bind the arms of the patient (or cursed one).
  To mark the "*usurtu*"[7] boundary with the sprinkling of lime."
  The "*usurtu*" must also be marked by the "*Flour of Nisaba*."

<u>Incantation of Ceremonial Affects</u>:
"At the head of these seven figures with the terrible wings ["fearful wings"], I have set a figure of NERGAL. I have conjured NUZKU ["*nusku*" the Fire-God] at their head in the [cauldron] – AGA MASS SSARATU. Twin figures ["guardians", "wards"] I have set to overwhelm the ["evil spirit"] at the right and left side of the ["sick", "possessed"] man. In the foundations of this place I have set the ["ward"] of LUGAL-GIRRA ["Lord of the Fires of GIBIL", "Lord of the Fires of Heaven-God"] of which there is no rival. Beneath the bed [where lays the "injured"] I have set the figure of NARUDU, Sister of the Elder Gods [who is connected to both the IGIGI-Watchers and to ISTAR]. That no evil shall drawn near I set AMEL-DISPU and LAT-ARAG as ["guardians", "wards"] of the doorway, with HULDUPPU to banish the existing evils. Within the door I have charged the twin warr-iors of "lime" - and the Watchers shall guard the door on the right and on the left." [*End of Incantation.*]

<u>The Prerequisites</u>:
  ...to be performed by the "Pure Offspring of the Deep"

---

7 *Usurtu* – the "*mandala*" or "magick circle" of operations.

(meaning the abode of EA-ENKI) – else, the Sons of Marduk.

...eat what is good and drink what is sweet – allow nothing "evil" to drawn near against your watching. [This portion may have been a part of some incantation being directed to a "guardian spirit", not necessarily the priest.]

The Incantation:
...is the Incantation of MARDUK.[8]

The Magician:
...is the embodiment of MARDUK, N son of N, whose god is N. and whose goddess is N, in whose body the sickness lies.

The Performance:
...the incantation is spoken when the cattle come home and when the cattle go out.

* * *

MARDUK has seen him. [meaning, the "sick one"]
MARDUK has gone to the house of his father, ENKI.
MARDUK asked of ENKI: "The headaches, whence comes it?"
And ENKI responded: "You know it is from the [Underworld], my son."
MARDUK asked of ENKI: "What this ailing man has done, he knows not.
How may he be relieved from this [Underworld curse]?
And ENKI responded: "My son, what you do not know now, I cannot give you.
My knowledge has already been added to your own. Go now."
But before MARDUK departed, ENKI did divulge to him the secrets...

---

[8] Code for the "*Incantation of Eridu*" [Tablet Y-Series, etc.]

THE BURNINGS REVISITED

The words KAS.SA.PI and KAS.SAP.TI appear often in the Banishing and Exorcism tablets of Mesopotamia. The most common used transliteration of the Maqlu Tablets also uses the expressions *"lukassapi"* and *"kassapti"* (e.g. *"lukassapi u kassapti"*).[9]

Although GIRRA appears frequently and is thought to be a spiritual sentient entity in itself, the 'Council of Nabu-Tutu' work with MERODACH showed evidence for the literal "fire gods" to be GIBIL (and also NUSKU), but the expression of "GIRRA" should be more accurately be translated as "fire of god" - as in the fires that a "god would wield" themselves. This is very critical in reconstructing the tradition, because it changes the implication of many of the lines found in the Mardukite Maklu Tablets.[10]

For example, the line given:

> GIRRA su.ta.bil.su.nu.ti[11]

Should *not* be accepted as:

> "Fire-God carry them away."

It should be interpreted as:

> "Fire of God, carry them away."

---

9 *Lukassapi u kassapti* – "the evil sorcerer and evil sorceress."
10 See the "M-Series" Tablets.
11 *Maqlu Tablet II line 115* – ("M-Series" Tablets).

Another example that we find in the M-Series giving the Babylonian transliteration of "An Incantation Against the Ancient Ones and Their Worshipers"[12] - we adopted the common interpretation at first but were later corrected. In the lines of the Incantation, practitioners will frequently lend a hand to the mind in connecting obscure words with their intended meanings, including names. Thus, the name for a deity is usually all that we have on a tablet, leaving the remaining interpretation up to the translator.

For example:

"GIRRA, Lord of the Flames,
       sears and burns you to the core."

In the above passage, the tablet says nothing about the "Lord of the Flames" - the tablet indicates "d-girra"[13] which is translated to 'GIRRA'. In the following line, both the "spirit" of "GIRRA and GIBIL [GI-BEL]" are called to "lend me power". Consider the following "mardukite" transliteration from the M-Series (here given also in English):

104. *EN dgirra a.ri.ru mar da.nim qar.du*
       Flaming Spirit GIRRA, Fires born of ANU
105. *iz.zu ahemes.su at.ta*
       Fiercest among your brethren
106. *sa ki.ma d.nanna u d.samas ta.da.an.nu di.i.nu*
       Bring the Judgment of NANNA and SAMAS
107. *di.i.ni di.ni puruss.ai purusus*
       Be the Jury of my case – Judge of the Decision
108. *qu.mi kas.sa.pi u kas.sap.ti*
       Burn the ("my") evil sorcerer and evil sorceress

---

12 From the *Schlangekraft Recension*.
13 *d-girra* – dingir-GIRRA or ilu-GIRRA, denoting divinity.

109. *dgirra qu.mu lukassapi u fkassapti*
 GIRRA, burn the evil sorcerer and evil sorceress
110. *dgirra qu.li lukassapi u fkassapti*
 GIRRA, consume the evil sorcerer and sorceress
111. *dgirra qu.mi.su.nu.ti*
 GIRRA, burn them now!
112. *dgirra qu.li.su.nu.ti*
 GIRRA, consume them now!
113. *dgirra ku.su.us.su.nu.ti*
 GIRRA, overpower ["overwhelm"] them now!
114. *dgirra a.ru.uh.su.nu.ti*
 GIRRA, destroy ["annihilate"] them now!
115. *dgirra su.ta.bil.su.nu.ti*
 GIRRA, carry them away immediately!

Mesopotamian tablets are used by the priests to counter the actions made by the "wicked magick-users" in the land, especially when they have made a specific person their target. The underlying intention behind these rites becomes clear: to appeal to the Higher Powers of which is also the source of the Evil Sorcerer's magick, to cut them off from that source by the pious appeal to the ANUNNAKI races, and finally the "belittlement" or "dispersal" of their energies, often "washed away in waters" or, as can be seen often in the Burning Rites, "incineration by fire."

In Babylon and among the Mardukite cult, mystical objects would be used by the priests for ceremonies of offering (appeasing the gods) and healing sickness or curses (petition to the gods). These objects often bore the names of deities, especially the Supernal Trinity of ANU, ENLIL and ENKI. Though not necessarily connected to the same three is the Sun, Moon and Venus that appear fundamental in the pictorial tablet depictions, including a "winged disc" that is not thought to represent anything in our solar system.

In addition to the more familiar *zonei* of the Babylonian system, the ancients adhered to a different "Ninurtian" hierarchy prior to the sealing of the Younger ANUNNAKI by MARDUK. Historians actually refer to them as the "Seven Ninurtas" (trans. "A.DAD" in some systems). They are:

1. URA'S of Dilbat
2. NINURTA of Nippur
3. ZABABA of Ki's(h)
4. NABU of Borsippa
5. NERGAL of Kutha (also spelled "Cutha")
6. MARDUK of Babylon (also "Mad-ANU")
7. PABILSAG of Isin

The afflictions of the people are recognized by the priest as a "spiritual entity" or "daemon" – whether or not they are self-induced (by obsess-ion or uncleanliness) or brought on by another (the "wicked" person). It may be that this belief makes the "exorcising" of sickness easier from a mystic perspective (e.g. "sympathetic magic").

While the true function of "spiritual atonement" may have been threshed out of "western religion" – it would seem that the practice of this is not only vital for "curing" but essential for the regular maintenance of physical wellbeing.

Combative magick (magical warfare) seems "fire oriented" given the concept of immolating the wickedness that has been "sent to" a target. But what of the poor soul who has become the victim of a different "curse" or "illness", one fated by the "gods" whereby some social or cleanliness taboo has been broken. For this we have "atonement" - which carries a root meaning: "to wash away", therefore removing the sickness that has been "summoned to" a being, knowingly or not.

In fact, the "Surpu" Tablet series carries with it a considerable list of "sins" or "taboos" that a person may have committed by accident, thus resulting in "casual" illness or affliction. For example, let us toy with the notion that the original "crab apple" tree was in fact the ancient Tree of Life in the Garden of E.DIN – the taboo placed upon such for Adam and Eve was not to eat it. But why?

What do we know about these kinds of fruits now that we might not have then?

Well – the apples, and all related fruits including cherries and peaches (etc.) actually contain the ingred-ients for cyanide poison – in the seeds! Now, swallowing a couple will probably do nothing noticeably – but chewing several of them... this can actually kill you!

Considering many of the ancient taboos including unclean sexual relations with animals, drinking water from a poor source or coming into contact with an environment or person that may be a contagion for disease, it almost makes good sense that the physical and observable consequences of such would lead to a belief in "sin" (originally the name for NANNA – the lunar Anunnaki god) and "divine curses" for such actions. This concept is actually put forth by many metaphysical and mystical scholars who believe that the "bans" and "tabus" of the ancient world were instilled in the people by a "higher" source that seemed to just "know better."

Curiously, a charm from the Surpu Tablets (Akkad-Babylonian) appear in the fore-front instructions for the rite of the AA (or Argentum Astrum) called the "Stele of Revealing" in the instructions for "Casting the Circle":

> Ban! Ban! Ban!
> Barrier that none shall pass!
> Barrier of the Gods, that none may break!
> Barrier of Heaven and Earth,
> The Bond unchangeable.
> That no god may amend,
> And no god or man shall break free.

For the closing, the Egyptian form of MAAT [Word of Truth, Word of Power] is evoked as a means of clearing:

> IPSOS.
> Breath of the Universe, Soul of the Realm.
> MAAT – speak the Word of Truth (east)
> MAAT – share the Light of Justice (south)
> MAAT – lead the Way of Balance (west)
> MAAT – heal the Order of the Realm (north)
> MAAT – above me (heights)
> MAAT – below me (depths)
> MAAT – ["encompassing"] all things (center).
> Come Forth and be the Fire in my Heart.
> Come Forth and be the Life of my Future.
> Come Forth and let the Magickal Child be born.
> ABRAHADABRA.

Finally, the continuation of the first charm is as follows:

> A snare ["net"] without escape, set for "evil"
> A net which none can control to spread evil.
> Whether it be the evil genius, daemon or ghost,
> Or the evil devil, evil god or evil fiend,
> Or hag-demon, ghoul, or thieving-sprite,
> Or wraith, nightmare, or mistress of the night,
> Or evil plague, fever-sickness, or unclean disease.

What has attacked the shining waters of ENKI,
May the "net" of ENKI capture it;
Or whatsoever has spoiled the grains of NISABA,
May the "net" of NISABA combat it;
Or whatsoever has broken the sacred barrier,
Let the barrier of the gods be protected,
And the bond of heaven and earth, be free.
That which does not reverence the Elder Gods,
May the great gods trap it,
May the great gods curse it;
Whatsoever has attacked the house,
May the great gods cast it into an enclosure;
Or whatsoever swirls circles round and round to confuse,
May the great gods cast it into a place with no escape;
Or whatsoever the gets closed into the house by the door,
May the great gods cast it into a house with no exit;
Or whatsoever slips past the bolted door,
May the great gods ever keep hold over it with a bolt.
That which blows into the household at the crevices,
Or that which forces its way through the latch,
Like the waters may it pour out from that place,
Like a glass cup may it be thrashed into pieces,
Like a delicate tile may it be broken so easily.
Or whatsoever makes its way over the wall,
May the great gods cut off its wings;
Or whatsoever finds a way to hide in the rooms,
May the great gods cut its throat;
Or whatsoever sneaks to steal a glance of the rooms,
May the great gods force out its eyes;
Or whatsoever mutters curses quietly in the dwelling,
May the great gods force its mouth shut forever;
Or whatsoever roams free in the attics,
May the great gods conceal it in the "between";
Or whatsoever darkens the dawn,
May the great gods imprison it in the "place of sunrise."

MARDUKITE MEDICINE, CURSES & ATTONEMENT

As has been expressed implicitly throughout Mardukite literature, the role of MARDUK in Babylon and Egypt was to surpass the more primitive religions (including those pretending to be monotheistic) in dedication to other ANUNNAKI who sought to enslave mankind, keeping them removed in ignorance from the Source in a Realm of Darkness, much of it originating not of malignant expressions, but necessity for the system-design of the reality matrix.[14]

MARDUK is unique in the position among the "gods" in that he has the power (granted once by the "fifty names") to supersede them and their decisions in the Material Realm. We see evidence for this again in the "Surpu" tablets which lists "sins" or "taboos" as MAM.IT. In one part we find:

> The MAMIT of any kind that afflicts a man,
> MARDUK, Priest of the Gods, can attend.

In this case, we translate it to apply to sickness specifically, choosing the words "afflict" and "attend". An alternative to this would be to liken the situation to a curse that has been placed on the person for violating some MAMIT, thus replacing the above two words with "curse" or "binding" and "loosen". Several lines of the third tablet of the *Surpu Series* are spent in listing the deities whose powers MARDUK can actual undo! And its pretty impressive:

---

14 See also *Liber-R* ('*Necronomicon Revelations*' also available in the Mardukite Year-2 *Liber-50+51+R* anthology '*Gates of the Necronomicon*').

> MARDUK can loosen the MAMIT of ANU and ANTU, BEL [ENLIL] and BELIT, ENKI and DAMKINA, NANNA and NINGAL, SAMAS and AA, ADAD and SALA, [MARDUK and SARPANIT], NABU and TASMIT, NINIB...

It essentially burns through the entire pantheon! In addition, MARDUK is hailed *"musim simate sa ilani kalama"* – the one who determines [holds] the fates [destiny?] of the gods, though some scholars believe this role to be purely cyclic (connected to the zodiacal ages), or revolving among the ANUNNAKI – the Mardukite lore would suggest otherwise – that the Younger God gained immediate respect among his Elders by doing "what you ANUNNAKI could not have."

On an Assyrian tablet used for healing, the god SAMAS is evoked as "Chief of the Gods". The *Spirit of Merodach* has made the connection for us too, that SAMAS is AZAZEL (Azazil = عزازل) - a being also connected to the Wild Goat God of the Woods (ENKI), for too, consider Leviticus where Aaron "casts lots" upon two goats, one for the Lord (BEL) and one for AZAZEL (SAMAS). The goat selected by the Lord is sacrificed as a sin offering – but the goat to SAMAS is to be presented while still living to the Lord, "to make atonement over it" and then it is set free into the wilderness (apparently the wild domain of AZAZEL). That AZAZEL-SAMAS actually appears frequently in Judeo-Christian scriptures in relation to the *"Day of Atonement."*

The Assyrian Tablet reads:

> By the MAAT [power word of truth] of ENKI
> May this man, the son of his god N.,
> Become pure, clean and bright among things.

> May this man be cleansed like a vessel of fat [lard, oil],
> May this man be cleansed like a vessel of butter [etc.].
> Unto SAMAS, Chief of the Gods, commend him,
> By SAMAS, Chief of the Gods,
> May this man's welfare be protected [secured, sealed]
> By the hands of the ANUNAKI ["gods"].

This Assyrian text – and similar appeals to the Higher – are very like, in nature and intent, to the actual Hebrew prayer that accompanies the goat-atonement rite – it should be clear that ENLIL is actually thought to be the wrathful Lord of the Old Testament Hebrew:

> Lord, I have acted iniquitously,
> I have trespassed and sinned before You;
> I, my household, and the sons of Aaron,
> Your holy [sacred, good] race.
> O Lord, forgive the iniquities,
> Forgive the transgressions and sins that
> I, my household, and the sons of Aaron,
> The holy people dedicated to You,
> As is written in the law of Moses, Your servant:
> "On this day He will forgive you,
> To cleanse you from all your sins before the
>   Lord; Ye shall be clean."

According to the Book of Enoch, AZAZEL is the Chief of the Grigori, another word for "fallen angels" or "Anunnaki,"[15] though the modern Semitic version would leave us with the impression to liken this being to a generic "*Satan*" – the

---

15 *Anunnaki* – trans. "fell to earth from heaven" by Zecharia Sitchin; trans. "decree fate on earth" by Mardukite Research Organization.

"warrior" nature is what is actually called upon by MARDUK in the construction of the weapons used to kill KINGU and TIAMAT. In the Book of Enoch, after the "Sons of God" fall and then interbreed with the "Daughters of Men"...

> AZAZEL taught men to make swords, knives, shields and breastplates; and made known to the people the natures of the earthly metals and the art of working them properly; and the natures of bracelets and ornamentation of the body and the beautification of the eyes and face; with all manners of precious stones and coloring tinctures. And there arose much godlessness in the hearts of the people, for they had become vain with their knowledge and committed acts of fornication now being that they were led astray had they easily become completely corrupted in their ways.

With the physical sway of MARDUK become unseen with the passage of time – all but to be forgotten – it is the "Sun-King" or "Sun-God" - a warrior spirit among the gods – who makes a more central appearance in the relatively more recent practices of paganism. Keeping in mind the words, "God", "Heaven", "Planet" and "Star" are essentially synonymous in the Mesopotamian paradigm, we can see that this concept is somewhat confusing to the primitive mind that evolved from it (given the loss of sacredness and pure – self honest – meaning being removed from religion over the last few thousand years...).

In the following rite, a dead man is to be buried in the ground – all of his personal affects are to be washed (cleansed with water) – and a figure is made in his image to also be buried so as not to incite the visitation of his spirit thereafter. The burial hymn is dedicated to SAMAS or an equivalent solar-god name:

> SAMAS, King of Heaven and Earth,
> Judge of what is Above and Below,
> Lord of the Dead – Ruler of the Living.
> SAMAS, the Dead have risen and appeared,
> The *"edimmu"*[16] of my father and mother,
> The *"edimmu"* of my brother or my sister,
> Let them accept the worldly death and be free.

---

16 *Edimmu* – traditionally translated as "ghost" or "ancestral spirit."

DEVILS & DEMONS OF BABYLON
(FEVERS, EVIL SPIRITS & HEADACHES)

It is curious to the present editor that it was in the first decade of the 20th Century that so many of the tablets of the ancients came under public attention, translated from their original cuneiform by some extraordinary and adventurous minds – most of them not even realizing what part they were playing. For that matter we might say that the Gates began to crack open for this "NO AGE" at the same time – for at the same time the magics of the Semitics, Sumerians, Babylonians, Akkadians and Assyrians had begun to be explored for the public – Aleister Crowley was in Egypt discerning secrets that would begin the Armageddon Clock of humanity. Now – for a century, few but the elite have even dared explore the mysteries, shrouding it in gloom, dangers and fears innumerably connected to the same horrifying images of cthonic gore. The mysteries are being revealed to the current generation – lest they be forgotten.

* * * * * * *

Using the hair of a "virgin child", a "wise woman" must spin it "double" [twice thick] to make a rope. Bind twice seven [fourteen] knots. Perform the *"Incantation of Eridu."*[17]

> Bind the head of the sick man. Bind the neck of the sick man. Bind the life of the sick man. Bind the limbs of the sick man.

Encircle the couch [bed, etc.] the man lays in with the "Waters of the Incantation" ["holy water" or water blessed by

---

17 *Incantation of Eridu* – Mardukite Pentagram Rite (Y-Tablets).

the priests incantations prior] – and may the headache ascend to heaven as the smoke of the incense of purification. And like the waters that rain down on the lands, may the headache be seeped deep in the "beneath" - returning to the Underworld in which it was born. The incantation of finality (a prayer of amen, "it is finished" or "so mote it be") used in the exorcising rites:

ZI DINGIR ANNA [ANU] KANPA
By the Heavens you are exorcised, so conjure [be] it!
ZI DINGIR KIA KANPA
By the Earth you are exorcised, so conjure [be] it!
BAN BAN BAN – By the Gods I conjure an impassable
    barrier!
By the Heavens I conjure an impassable blockade!
By the Earth I conjure an impassable bridge!
By the Heavens and Earth, Powers of Light and Darkness,
I conjure the binding that none shall break!
No God shall annul – No man shall change!
A net without escape – which cannot be used for evil.

    [restored ending to the prayer of finality]

Amat EA lisu dingir damgal nunna heensidi [...]
May the word [MAAT] of ENKI make clear [passage for
    me],
DAMKINA liste y sir dingir silig elim nun na dusag
    zuabge sagga tagtaglibi zaakan,
May DAMKINA guide us with the light of the
    Truth, and the Eldest Son of the Deep,
MARDUK mdru rtsiuu sa apsii buunnuu duummiiku
MARDUK, thine is the power to brighten and bless.

    * * * * * * *

An evil spirit is prevalent in the land.
It torments the people both above and below.
It is a pestilence, a plague with no rest.
It wishes desolation for all wherever it goes.
The Great Demon – The Great Spirit – The Great Fiend
That which roams where the multitudes gather.
The angry fierce quaking storm that thrashes about.
Like the pestilence in the streets,
Which NERGAL had brought.
It is not I, but MARDUK who performs the incantations.

CAUSES OF HEADACHE, DISEASE & POSSESSION
[According to the "Surpu" Tablet Series]

The person who has...
    ...sinned against his God.
    ...sinned against his Goddess.
    ...performed the unknown sin against his God.
    ...performed the unknown sin against his Goddess.
    ...misconducted himself before the God.
    ...misconducted himself before the Goddess.
    ...made his God and Goddess angry with him.
    ...sought undue secrets of the Gods of Heaven.
    ...sought undue secrets of the Temple-Shrines of
        Earth.
    ...slighted what is due to the Gods.
    ...sought undue favor of the Gods at the Temple-
        Shrines.
    ...offered impure sacrifice at the Altar of
        Offering.
    ...offered sacrifice to the [Gods] and taken it back.
    ...destroyed the sacrifice made at the Altar of
        Offering.
    ...obstructed the sacrifices made by another.

...caused obstruction between comrades [friends, family].
...eaten the flesh of a sacrifice at the Altars of Offering.
...held hatred towards an elder.
...shed his neighbor's blood.
...propositioned their neighbor's wife.
...propositioned their neighbor's husband.
...used a false balance in business affairs.
...removed or misplaced a boundary or landmark.
...unjustly entered their neighbor's house.
...taken their neighbor's garment.
...stolen or caused another to steal.
...said "no" for "yes" and "yes" for "no" [lying].
...been straight in the mouth but not true in the heart.
...promised pleasure and joy but not given it.
...spoken of what is unholy.
...spoken wickedness.
...caused a judge to receive a bribe.
...wronged his city.
...opposed one in authority under MARDUK.
...give in small things but refused in great.
...transgressed the righteous.
...offended the righteous.
...set their hand to evil acts.
...set their hearts to follow after evil.
...stopped a neighbor's canal [water supply].
...been banned of weapons but seeks them.
...set his hand to evil sorceries and witchcraft.
...pointed at the holy fire.
...taken a prolonged seat in the sun [sun-stroke].
...struck the young of an animal.
...tearing up plants in the desert.
...tearing of plants and trees.

...raised a fire and falsely sworn by a god.
...has tasted from the unclean cup.
...has tasted from the unclean plate.
...has tasted from the unclean dish.

**MARDUKITE
CHAMBERLAINS**

– Mardukite "Liber-9" Amethyst Tablet Collection –

THE BOOK OF AL-JILWAH

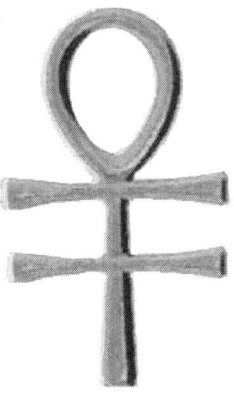

Tablet-J Series

– Mardukite "Liber-9" Amethyst Tablet Collection –

**MARDUKITE
CHAMBERLAINS**

THE BOOK OF AL-JILWAH & MELEK-TA'US

Few occultists who remain in the Light are probably privy to lore of the ancient Yezidi sect. They follow a tradition dedicated to the "God of the Black Mountain" who gave to them wisdom in what is known as the oldest of the "Black Books". While the Realm of Light has shied away from such – or believed they have attained more than a glimpse of it in their "Books of Shadows", it is this Divine Encounter that has been omitted from traditional biblical tales for its connections and devotion to the Darkness.

The Yezidi are a distinct genetic Mesopotamian sect that still resides in Northern Iraq and can trace its blood and traditions to the ancient ANUNNAKI quite easily. It is a unique form of Mardukite Monotheism presented under the guise of a messenger named Melek Ta'us (very similar to the manifestation of MARDUK as Mithras and Mazda – as One – in the Zoroastrian schema.[18] This same current of energy is also manifest in Maitreya for Buddhists.

In accordance with the Yezidic Tradition, there is an All-Father or YAZDAN who created the Seven ANUNNAKI ("emissaries" or "angels") including Azazel (or Azazil – perhaps also equated with Azrael). The word "Azif" and the actual book, "Al Azif", is a Yezidic tome detailing the lore, or literally "howls" of the Djinns (or jinn).

Some scholars of the *Necronomicon*-Cycle will note that one of the popular Arabic translations for the title of the work is, in fact, *Al Azif*.[19] The reason for this being that there were

---

18 Noted in the "S-Series" and "Z-Series" tablets.
19 Also named for the sound of the "buzzing of insects."

no other ancient examples of such a tome known to exist in that region – and to our gain, the lore compliments the existing ANUNNAKI based Mardukite NECRONOMICON even further. The association with the "buzzing of insects" could be meant to mean both the "swarm" and the "sound," furthering the connection of the *Outer Ones* with "UFO" extraterrestrial beings.

The seven deities or "Great Gods" created by YAZDAN are connected to, as we might expect, both the seven-star constellation of Ursa Major – *the Great Bear* – but also the seven visible "stars" of the ancient world, that of the ANUNNAKI *Zonei*. In addition to Chaldean lore suggesting the origins of the zodiacal wheel to be a chart for the age of rulership of the twelve-fold ANUNNAKI of the "Older Pantheon" of "Elder Gods" - it is the seven-fold schema of the "Younger Pantheon" that we see become dominant during the more relatively recent Babylonian era. The Yezidic lore suggests that each of these seven figures is given reign of the material kingdom in turn, marked by an age of 10,000 years.

Curious to Yezidi culture, though not exceptionally unique when compared to other lore of Dragonblood and ANUNNAKI Kings, is that the Yezidis claim to share Adamic (from "Adam") descent but not of Eve. Their lore also prompts that the remaining global population outside of their sect is also outside of this "special" lineage. And to them, they were given "Revelation" (*"Al-Jilwah"*) from their Divine Encounters with a being who the Judeo-Christians denoted as *Satan* (and perhaps others might liken to ENKI). It might be said that based on the purest use of the term, the Yezidi represent the oldest "Satanists" on the planet – if such were even possible in pre-Semitic times.

QU'RET AL-YEZID
THE REVELATION OF MELEK-TA'US

My knowledge encompasses the very Truth of all that Is,
And My wisdom is not separated from My Source,
The Manifestation of My [blood] descent is clear unto you,
And when it is Revealed to the Children of Adam it will
      become as a Sword of Fire among the multitudes,
And many will tremble thereby.

All habitations (especially the desert spaces) are of
My own creation, programs I have set into action,
All completely from within My own strength,
And not the result of the false gods;
Wherefore I am He that men should rightly worship,
Not the false gods of their books, wrongly written;
      Poorly remembered.

But they come to know Me, a Peacock of bronze and of gold,
My Wings spread over the [Kaba] Temple and Church, not
      to be overshadowed.

And in the secret cave of My wisdom it is known:
I am the Voice of God; there is no God but Myself,
      [An Archangel commanding legions,
      Melek Ta'us.

Knowing this, who would dare deny Me?
Knowing this, who would dare fail to worship Me?
Knowing this, who would dare to continue the
      worship of false idols found in the Koran and Bible?
Knowing this, who shall make that effort to no ends?

But know this: that he who knows Me,
I may cast into pleasure-filled gardens of Paradise!
But the Yezid who chooses to not know Me,
I will make death, as life, one-thousand afflictions.

Proclaim then, I am the only Archangel to be exalted;
And I will make prosperous whom I wish to rest my Eye,
And I will enliven those I choose to rest my Hand.
Proclaim then, I alone am to be praised of the
Seven Towers [*Pillars*] of the ANUNNAKI,
My Name shall be heard from the Mountain of Ararat to the
        Western Sea.

Proclaim then, Let the Light of True Knowledge flash
        forth from the Ziarahs [*Seraphim, Zonei or Satans*],
Flash forth from the rivers of the Euphrates
And the Tigris [the boundaries of Mesopotamia] to the
hidden folds of Shambalah.

Let My Kingdom be carried from its safe place into the
        Temple,
And let the Yezidi know Me by My Manifestations,
Even Sheikan, Sinjar, Haliteyeh, Malliyeh, and Lepcho,
        [*a series of esoteric proper names are given*]
And the Kotchar [another obscure name] who wander
        among the heathens [*savage unsaved multitudes*].

MESHAF I-RESH – BLACK BOOK OF MELEK-TA'US

In the beginning was the Invisible One [God]
Who brought forth the White Pearl,
From out of His own precious Essence.

He then brought forth a bird into being named Anfar.
And on its back He placed the White Pearl,
And there it rested for forty thousand years.

Then, on the first day, Sunday,
He created an Archangel over all angels [*sky-gods*]
Named 'Ezrail', which is Melek Ta'us, the Peacock Angel,
    [*also "Azrael-Michael" or "Marduk"*]
The First-to-Be, the chief of all.

Each subsequent day, an angel to serve Melek Ta'us.
On Monday, Dardael came forth, who is Sheikh Hasan.
On Tuesday Izrasel came forth, who is Sheikh Shams.
On Wednesday, Jibrael [Gabriel - GIBIL] came forth,
    who is Sheikh Abu-Bekr [AIQ BKR]
On Thursday, Azrael, who is Sajadin, came forth.
On Friday, Shemnael came forth, who is Nassurud-Din.
On Saturday Nurael, who is Zuriel, came forth.
    Melek Ta'us was chief over them all.

When after all this had been done,
The Invisible One [*God*] returned to its abode, and acted no
    more.
From this point, Melek Ta'us was left to act alone.

First he moved to separate the heavens by seven [*Zonei*],
And also a veil for the earth, sun, and moon.

Seeing the barrenness of the realms,
He created humans, animals, various birds and beasts,
Placing them in the between spaces accompanied by angels.

Melek Ta'us stood before the White Pearl and shouted.
It was broken into four pieces.
He commanded Gabriel to take two of the pieces;
One was placed beneath the earth, and the other was
    placed at the Gate of Heaven.

The other two pieces were placed in the sun and the moon,
And the stars were created from their fragments,
Suspended in heaven for the delight of the [gods].

The Mighty Lord Melek Ta'us spoke:
"O angel brethren, I will to create the Adam and Eve,
  And I will make them human beings, and from them
  two shall arise, out of the loins of Adam, Shehr
  ibn Jebr; and from him shall arise a single people
  on the earth: The Yezidi people."

Then Melek Ta'us commanded Gabriel to come forth
And take parts from the four corners of the world: the
    elements: earth, air, fire and water.
He man from the four and instilled a fragment of Divine
    Spark in each, a "soul" given by his power.

Gabriel was commanded to place Adam in the Gardens of
    Paradise [E.DIN],
Where he was permitted to eat fruit of every green herb,
Only wheat was he commanded not to eat.

After a hundred years Ta'us Melek went to God asking:
"How shall Adam increase and multiply, and where are his
    offspring?"

God replied to him: "This is not my concern. Into your
 hands I have given it."

Melek Ta'us then asked of Adam: "Have you eaten the
 wheat?"
And Adam answered: "No, I am forbidden to do so."
Melek Ta'us then said to him: "It would behoove you to eat
 of the wheat."

So, Adam ate of the wheat.
But, after he had eaten, his stomach swelled up.

Ta'us Melek drove him out of Paradise [E.DIN], and left him
 alone, ascended into the heavens disgusted.

Adam suffered from the pains in his stomach, because his
 waste had no outlet.
God blessed Adam by sending a bird,
Which helped him by making an outlet for Adam's relief.
 (Though some say the bird was Gabriel trans-
 formed.)
Eve was then created from beneath Adam's left arm-pit.

Melek Ta'us descended to the earth,
Returning for the sake of our people [the Yezidis]
And he brought kings to rule alongside the ancient kings
 (of the Assyrians);
Nesrukh, who is Nassurud-Din [*Nasiru'd-Din*] and
Kamush, who is King Fakhru'd-Din and Artimus, who is
 King Shamsu'd-Din.
And when after these had ruled, we had two kings,
The first and second Persian Shapurs,
Who are Mazdayasnians of AHURA-MAZDA,
And whose rule was given to last one hundred and fifty
 years.

From this tree has brought us the seed of our Amirs [AMAR
    or "chieftain ruler"]
Through to the present day; And we in turn became
    divided.

Know that it is not permitted to utter the name
    SHAITAN – because it is the name of God.

Nor should any name be spoken that resembles this,
    Such as Kitan, Sharr and Shatt;
Nor also any vocalization resembling Malun, Malek or Nayl.

In the time before the Common Era,
Our religion was called idol-worship:
  and the Jews, Christians, Muslims and Persians steered
  clear from our traditions.

King Ahab and Amran were among our own,
  and they have named the God of Ahab, BEELZEBUB, whom
  they have also called among us, Pirbub.
We had a king from among our own in BABYLON;
  whose name was Bukhti-Nossor [*Nebuchadnezzer*],
And Ahasuerus in Persia was among our own,
And in Constantinople, Aghriqalus was among our own.

              * * * * * * *

Know too the secret:
  When first before heaven and earth had been made,
  The Lord was suspended over the waters,
  In a chariot above the waters, He was suspended.

Then the Lord ascended into the heavens,
    and the heavens were condensed for His
        existence and fixed the heavens to exist
            without supports.

Then the earth was condensed and sealed away from it.

From His own Divine Essence [*sparks of light*],
He created the six [*gods*] to be like the light of a lamp,
Each successively lighting off the light of the other.

And he said to the first: "Ascend!
And create something else apart from you."
And the Moon [*Gate-Zonei*] came into being,
   and so began the succession of the Spheres [*gods*].

KITAB AL-JILWAH
THE SERMON OF REVELATION

This is the Book of Al-Jilwah recording a true and faithful communic-ation from the God, Melek Ta'us, who existed before all other creatures on earth. He has sent his servant messenger into this world to guide and separate his chosen people from their errors [sins]. The texts which follow are the account first made to the faithful servants via an oral tradition – but the Lord allowed the book of *Al-Jilwah* to be written before him, so long as no strangers to the Yezidi would behold it.

****

1. I was, and am now, and will continue unto eternity, ruling over all creatures and ordering the affairs and deeds of those who are under my command. [*Omnipotence*]

2. I am presently available to those who trust in me and call upon me in time of need, neither is there any place void of me where I am not capable of presence. [*Omnipresence*]

3. I am involved in the natures of all those things which strangers call evil only because they are not according to their own desire. [*Freedom – Civil Disobedience*]

4. Every Aeon [age] has a Ruler [regent who is under my counsel – Every generation changes their natures by the Chief [Lord] of this World, so that each one of them has his turn and cycle to fulfill his charge. [*Zodiacal Age*]

5. I grant indulgences freely but according to the merits of those qualities which is laden in the disposition of the nature. [*Karmic Law of Returns*]

6. He who opposes me shall experience grievous regret.

7. No other gods may interfere in my business and work: whatsoever I determine, that is what will be.

8. The Scriptures which are in the hands of strangers, even though they were written by prophets and apostles, others have turned the truth of these aside, and rebelled, and perverted them; and each one of them confuses the other and all are lost to it.

9. Truth and Falsehood are distinguished by proving them at the time of their inception.

10. I will fulfill my promise to those who put their trust in me, those will uphold the covenant of the Ancient of Days, and also to those who act contrary to it, by accordance of the judgment made by the wise or my Rulers [*Regents*] that I delegate to execute my authority for me while on earth.

11. I take notes of all affairs, and promote the performance of what is deemed useful [*good*] in its due time.

12. I direct and teach those who will actually follow my teaching, who find with me joy and delight by natural accord far greater than any worldly joy.

13. I choose to reward and punish the progeny of Adam by all different manners of which I have knowledge.

14. I hold in my hand the means to control the earth and what is above and below it.

15. I do not concern myself much with the other races, but neither do I withhold good from them; much less do I begrudge it to those who are my chosen people and obedient servants to hold prejudice.

16. I will surrender active worldly control into the hands of those proven, in accordance with my will, to be friends in some shape and fashion to such as they are faithful and abide by my counsel.

17. Indeed, I take and I give; I can make rich and I can make poor; happy and wretched, all in accordance to the natural environments and seasons [*cycles*], of which there are none who have the right to interfere, or to withdraw man from the system I control.

18. I bring down pain and sickness upon those who strive to thwart me.

19. He who is recorded as mine shall not experience death like other men.

20. I deem that no man should dwell in this lower world for more than the period prescribed by me; and, if I wish it, I will send him back into this world a second and a third time (or more) by way of the trans-migration of the soul, and such exists by a universal law.

21. I guide you without a scripture to be profaned and point to you the way by an unseen hand, though my friends and such will recognize me in my teachings and can be found by their observation of the precepts, which is not a laborious accord and will adapt itself to time and cultures as needed.

22. I punish those who do not adhere to the laws also in other worlds.

23. The children of Adam don't know the Secrets of Destiny [*Fate, Union*] and so they fall to error in their beliefs and followed actions.

24. I control the beasts of the field and the birds of the heaven and the fish of the sea, as all of them are in my hand.

25. All of the secret treasures and wondrous hoards buried deep in the heart of the earth are known to me, and I can cause one after another to inherit these riches on earth.

26. I make visible [*manifest*] my signs and wonders [*miracles*] to those who will receive them and self-honestly seek them from me in their due season [*time, cycle*].

27. The opposition of strangers to me and my followers do nothing except injure my cause – and know that they will be dealt with as is deserving.

28. The ordering of the spheres [*heavens, worlds*], the revolution of the Aeons [*ages, cycles*], and the changing of their Rulers [*Regents*] are mine from eternity [*Kingship has been descended from Heaven*].

29. Those who are not capable of reaching their appointed Destiny [*Fate, Union*], him I will chastise in my time [*age, Aeon*] and will cause him to relive his former charge.

30. The seasons of the Material Kingdom are four, and the elements are four; these have I maintained to secure the needs of my creatures.

31. The scriptures of strangers are accepted by me in so far as they accord and agree with my ordinances and do not contradict them; for they have been for the most part corrupted by mortal minds.

32. There are Three who are opposed to me, and these three names I hate above all else, and I shall not reveal [*possibly the Supernal Trinity of the ANUNNAKI*].

33. My promises are fulfilled to those who keep to the law.

34. Those who have undergone tribulations as martyrs for my sake will be compensated without fail in one of the worlds [spheres, heavens] in my domain.

35. It is my desire that all of my followers are united together on account that there are multitudes who are strangers to them and may band in opposition.

36. Those observing my law should reject teachings and dogma that are not from me.

37. Do not make mention of my name or my attributes [natures], as idle strangers do, or else be guilty of a sin by an ethic for which you have no knowledge of.

38. Honor my symbol and image, let the mark of it remind you of our covenant and of what has been neglected of my laws and ordinances.

39. Be obedient and attentive to my servants who are blessed by my Eye and Hand; listen to what they communicate to you of that knowledge of from the unseen which they have receive from me.

– Mardukite "Liber-9" Amethyst Tablet Collection –

THE BOOK OF QLIPPOTH

Tablet-Q Series

– Mardukite "Liber-9" Amethyst Tablet Collection –

MARDUKITE
CHAMBERLAINS

THE BOOK OF QLIPPOTH & THE OTHER SIDE

This close of the Year 1 cycle of Mardukite materials is meant to bridge what is in the "light" to what is laying hidden in the "shadows," in the "darkness," in the "night." O, Sons of the Night, gather around to hear the words which might bring you to the "Crossing to the Abyss" - that which you desire must strongly in your heart – your heart's desire.

* * * * * * *

The evil [fever] has set upon like a deluge,
Wide and broad it fills the whole of the Earth.
Enveloped in Terror, cloaked in Fear;
It roams freely about the streets...
It invisibly stands beside any man...
It sits and whispers to any man...
When it enters the home, its appearance is unknown.
When it goes forth out of the home,
It has gone unnoticed ["is not perceived"].

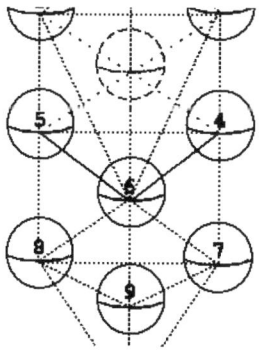

THE BROKEN FRAGMENT

It has been established, the Nations shall return to the
    Source.
Nations of men will return to the Womb of Creation.
To NIBIRU, Eternal Creatrix – Mother Goddess.

The ANUNNAKI have set forth the decree.
From the Heavens, the ANUNNAKI decree the fates for their
    creation.
From ANU is ENKI and ENLIL
From ENKI and ENLIL and NINHURSAG
Came the race to relieve the toil of the IGIGI [Watchers].

ENKI [PTAH], Founder of Men,
Founder of the Temple-Shrine in ERIDU,
ANU – Father of All.
Father of the Dynasty in BAD-TIBIRA,
Father of the Dynasty in LARSA,
Father of the Dynasty in SIPPAR and SHURUPAK.

Aye, the First Cities of Men,
Were founded by the ANUNNAKI,
Those who fell to the Earth from the Heavens,
They were the Light-Bearers among the Nations,
They were men of renown, revered among the Nations.

ANU, ENLIL, ENKI – Sent Messengers.
Multitudes poured forth from the Heavens [IGIGI, etc.]
Then, led by MARDUK – all evil was expelled.
The Divine Ordinances of the Temple-Shrines,
The Books of Knowledge and Rites,
These were entrusted to the priest-kings of men.

MARDUK & THE PLAGUE

May MARDUK, Eldest Son of ERIDU
Sprinkle the afflicted one with pure water,
Clean water – Bright water;
With the water, twice seven times,
That he may be pure, that he may be clean;
Let the evil RABISU Daemon go forth
And stand away from the afflicted one;
May a kindly SEDU [spirit],
May a kindly LAMASSU [guardian],
Come forth and be present near his body.

The priest is to make an image of the affected person in dough, so as to force the Plague-God that afflicts the person to come away from the body and into the image. The ancient tablets list the name of the Plague-God as NAMTARU, and in other places it may be found as URA. The texts continue:

Plague-God that devours the land like fire,
Plague-God that attacks the man like a fever,
Plague-God that roams the wind like a desert,
Plague-God that seizes the man like an evil thing,
Plague-God that torments like a pestilence,
Plague-God that has no hands or feet, but wanders the
    Night.
Plague-God that tears the afflicted man in shreds,
That binds the body of the afflicted man,
That has decreased the strength of the afflicted man,
Like a withering plant.
At night on his bed, the afflicted one cannot sleep.
The Plague-God has affected his body.

The Plague-God has seized his loins.
The god of the afflicted one is distant,
The goddess is far from the body.
MARDUK has set his eye on the body.
MARDUK has set his hand on the body.

Pull off a piece of clay from the "deep" - fashion an image of the afflicted one's form and place it in the loins of the sick man at night. At dawn, make atonement for the body and perform the Incantation of ERIDU [Mardukite Pentagram Rite],[20] turn his face to the west, that the evil Plague-God, the Great NAMTARU, wide with dread, which has seized the body of the afflicted one, will vanish away from him.

****

Square tablets have been found in the Middle East and elsewhere related to the secrets of the ANUNNAKI energetic "magicks" and protections offered to the priest-kings and children of MARDUK. These tablets were designed to be hung on a wall, particularly over doorways and thresholds. The origins of the "Peace-Love-Unity" [/|\-<3-8] triad used among the Ordo Nabu Maerdechai is actually derived from such a tablet, which is found to be a "mardukite" tablet complete with a visual depiction. From an antiquarian manuscript we have found the following with the words: "May the Temple-Shrine of ASSUR & MARDUK be over this house!"

---

20 *Incantation of Eridu* – see Tablet-Y Series.

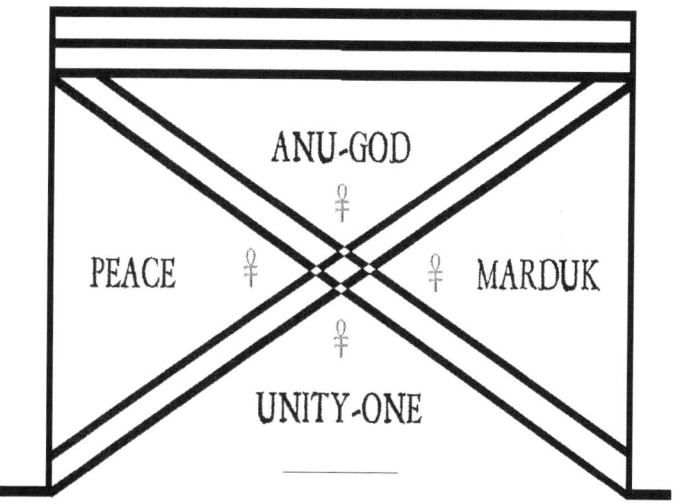

MARDUK went to his father for help,
To drive out the fever-daemon -
May pestilence be driven from the body.
ENKI advised him: "Fashion an image of his likeness
From dough and Earth - Set it upon the ground [holy
    ground]
Take men with a king [noble or literal] over him,
Take his hand before the "Sun" [SAMAS].
Repeat the incantation SAR-AZAG-GA
While pouring water of his head and the Incantation of
    ERIDU.

THE RITUAL OF THE HANGING STONES
SHADOW RITES FROM THE UNDERWORLD
(CTHONIC NECRONOMICON GNOSIS)

So once we have put our foot it in, all that remains is of course to dislodge the Gates. To unleash the mighty forces within and around us – to being back the ANUNNAKI and let them have their reign on the Earth. And it matters not which names and ideals we attach to this ideal so long as it is maintained in the hearts and thoughts of the dedicated.

****

Let us discuss first the Primary Elements involved, the primum mobium as it were – water and air, yet also the spaces between them – the Heights and the Depths and the spaces between them. You have heard the name of Cthulhu – that name which men have connected to the Crossings, to the Land of Kutha (or Cutha), to the Underworld – of KUTU-LU – Darkness and Shadow abounds the name of TUTU and the TUTU-LU or alter-ego [Shadow] of the TUTU[21] is what men have feared – and they know not its nature – it has simply been whispered out of the ethereal mists and remained unseen in the Realm of Light.

Know that the animal forms given over to minds as "gods" are but shadows of truth of the "gods" who have fragmented our beings as separate and distinct – and at first it had been decreed that the union of the two were to remain separate and distinct – the blending being taboo. This lore

---

21 *TUTU* – an epithet for NABU (son of MARDUK); also found as one of the 'Fifty Names' from the '*Enuma Elis*' [Tablet-F]. NABU as 'Thoth-the-Younger' (TUTU/Tahuti) for the 'Younger Generation' of Anunnaki, replacing NINGISHZIDA (brother of MARDUK) as 'Thoth-the Elder' (TUTU/Tahuti).

has existed concerning those among the Old Ones and Elder Gods that did come down to set themselves upon the "daughters of men" - though it has been written that they "corrupted" the women – we knoweth not the natures and minds of the gods.

What fierce beast waits for us at the Crossing to the Abyss – what monstrous visions will we be forced to behold? What is the nature of the Dweller at the Threshold? And in what names are we to know these by? For after climbing the Ladder of Lights and establishing the whole of the Light – what other motivation can there be except to enter into the Beyond? Perhaps one of the most fundamental of thoughts when considering the Gnosis of the *Necronomicon Cycle* is the reverberating echo of: "The Power of Man is the Power of the Ancient Ones."

> *. . . and he read the dreaded name:*
> *CTHULHU*
>
> *. . . and he read the dreaded name:*
> *ZKHORONZON*

It has been compared to the Lovecraftian semantics – that the Depths are likened to Cthulhu and the Heights are to Yog-Sothoth. While these names, among others invoked from that mythos, do not necessarily appear one-to-one with specific names on ancient tablets or from classical mythologies. The idea of a system (or belief paradigm) being so restricted as to require a specific verbiage to operate correcting, completely defies the infinitude of magickal ideals and metaphysical mysticism.

The Circle of Stone is a mystical representations of space and time, of course, *fragmented* space and *fragmented* time. The number and arrangement of the stones, just like the number of points indicated on a star (significant to a number of stars and not necessarily the point). The elemental entity? The Watchtowers? Yea, they are interconnected to the Four that are One and to the Stones in the physical world raised and named to them.

> In the element of Water, Three Stones to
> SYTH OOLOO
>
> In the element of Fire, Six Stones to
> SYTH ODOWOGG
>
> In the element of Air, Eight Stones to
> HRU SYTH
>
> In the element of Earth, Five Stones to
> SHUGNIGOTH

The interpretation of this, as some [OTO, AA] have arrived at, is the close sounds to the Lovecraftian entities, namely, - Cthulhu [SYTH OOLOO], Yog Sothoth or Ossadagowah [SYTH ODOWOGG], Hastur [HRU SYTH], Shub-Niggurath [SHOGNIGOTH]. Then one will be immediately inclined to draw other conclusions of formulae, such as:

> 3 : Binah – Saturn:
> Water, the Great Deep:
> KUTULU
>
> 6: Tiphareth – Sun:
> Fire, solar center, Beast 666:
> YOG-SOTHOTH
>
> 8: Hod – Mercury:
> Air, Winged Messenger:
> HASTUR
>
> 5: Geburah – Mars:
> Earth, Goat of 1000-Young:
> SHUB-NIGGURATH

For those not privy to the methods of old, the ceremonial formula is simple enough: the number of stones are indicative to the energetic current being fragmented and channeled from the whole. The circle, is as always, a holy mandala of the Universe – the inner circle may be indicative of a transitionary element (e.g. the water gate or sea shells) and the diameter too is usually reflective of the current. The stones are equally spaced and "named" as they are set out or marked (much as in the manner of the shamanic Medicine Wheel) – though all workings can also be done in the astral.

Lines of Power – forming seemingly "star-glyphs", run across the surface of the most holy *nemeton* [mandala] that has been erected by the Stones of the Ancients. They not only form an energetic boundary for the "circle" - but too they cross the surface meeting not only the practitioner in the center, but also sharing the amplified resonance with one another to aid in the building of and channeling of energetic powers. Traditionally the stones ["earth element"] are to be collected by [near] the sea ["water element"] by the light of the full moon ["lunar current"] = and the working is sealed with the Incantation of ERIDU [e.g. Mardukite Pentagram Rite].

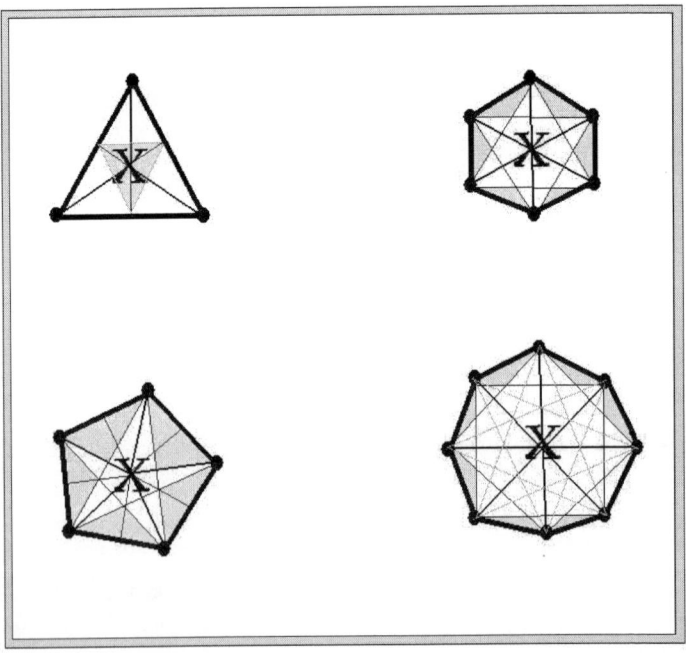

THE RITES AND LORE OF DAATH & LOVECRAFTIAN NECRONOMICON GNOSIS (SHADOWS FROM THE UNDERWORLD)

In the ancient and esoteric Semitic lore, there is a hidden sphere on the tree – a transitionary doorway occulted by the Light of the other Spheres – called Daath. It is the true 8th Sphere [Sephirot – Heaven or Gate] which is the height or summit of the material and also forms the basis and foundation (or depths) of the Supernal Triad – or Heights (whereby the Ninth Gate leads to the (Z)AIN).

****

AZATHOTH – The Primal Chaos, Center of Infinity, Formless, Unknown, the Anti-Thesis of Creation.
Zodiac: Leo; Direction: Hidden South
Alias: Azag-Thoth; Time Threshold: Sunday
Mardukite Pantheon: SAMAS (SHAMMASH-UTU)
Traditional Glyph: Spiral

YOG-SOTHOTH – All One – Unification – All in One, Vehicle of Chaos, Gate of the Void, Crossing to the Abyss.
Element: Fire; Zodiac: Leo
Direction: Immediate South; Time Threshold: Thursday
Mardukite Pantheon: MARDUK
Traditional Glyph: Circle

NYRALATHOTEP – Crawling Chaos, The Aether "Between" The Will of the "Old Ones" in "Space" [Outer Space] – Milky Way, the Tortuous Serpent or Path of the Serpent.
Alias: NyPaLa(t)hotep
Time Threshold: Wednesday
Mardukite Pantheon: NABU (NEBO)
Traditional Glyph: Wand of Power

HASTUR – Voice of the "Old Ones".
Element: Air
Zodiac: Aquarius
Direction: East Time Threshold: Saturday (?)
Mardukite Pantheon: NINIB ADAR
Traditional Glyph: Crescent

CTULU – Lord of "Deep Ones", Dreams, the Crossings of the Abyss.
Element: Water
Zodiac: Scorpio
Alias: Kutulu, Cthulu Direction: West
Time Threshold: Tuesday
Mardukite Pantheon: NERGAL
Traditional Glyph: Trapezoid

SHUB-NIGGURATH – The Black Goat, the Black Goat of the Woods (with 1000 Young), Gate of the North Wind.
Element: Earth
Zodiac: Taurus
Time Threshold: Friday
Mardukite Pantheon: ENKI (some list as ASTOR)
Traditional Glyph: Triangle

****

Make your invocation to Marduk and Sarpanit. Then call in (invoke) the Supernal Trinity – ANU, ENLIL and ENKI followed by a conjuration of the Fires and the Four Beacons ["lamps"] of the Watchtowers (cardinal directions). Performed the Incantation of ERIDU and call forth the presence of the personal Guardian-Spirit Watcher. Name the Talisman or Stone (whispering the name of the Seal or spirit called) and conduct the appropriate Invocation of the Gate.

– Mardukite "Liber-9" Amethyst Tablet Collection –

THE TABLETS OF INFORM

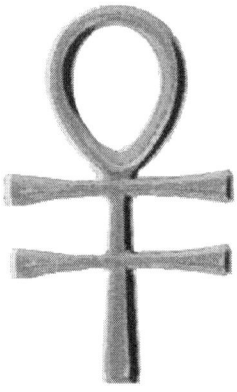

Tablet-I Series

– Mardukite "Liber-9" Amethyst Tablet Collection –

**MARDUKITE
CHAMBERLAINS**

THE TABLETS OF INFORM & CYPHER MANUSCRIPT

These which have been consolidated by the *Council of Nabu Tutu* of the *Ordo Nabu Maerdechai* in 2009 for the use of transliterating various texts, but primarily as guides or glimpses into another time-space, were incredibly useful in the interpretation of the M-Series Tablets[22] and other obscure works and incantations. Without the practitioner actually being able to speak the words with command and confide, they are meaningless. You end up in an occult 'catch-22' where you so seek to preserve the integrity of the system by intoning the words in a native language and yet at the same time have no idea what you are saying – even if you know the gist of it – still fail to fully tap the current desired.

It is without a question, absolutely true, that if you were to attempt the same work from a purely mystical standpoint the words and actions and such are without meaning because all is connected and you need not confine yourself to a single fragment of reality to experience this – but then, if you are going to be of this mind, then you would just as well do without the words altogether.

---

22 In 2009, the *Liber-N* materials 'Tablet-M' series were left as Akkadian (Babylonian) untranslated transliterations. These were not completed by the Mardukite Research Organization until 2011 and became the basis for *Liber-M* ('*Maqlu Magic*' or '*Necronomicon Spellbook II*' – also available in the complete Mardukite Year-3 *Liber-E+M+C* anthology '*Necronomicon Workbook*') and the 'Tablet-M' series was officially updated in 2012 for the revised and expanded fifth edition of the underground classic Mardukite Year-1 *Liber-N+L+G+9* anthology: '*Necronomicon Anunnaki Bible*'.

This is a book – a book of words – meant to also be a key to unlock other books and their words. Let those who have waited, be satisfied.

The plethora of nations that held sway over the ancient tablets each manipulated the language and interpretations to meet their own needs. This is fine and good except for when the historian has to recreate these factions thousands of years after the fact. The languages are very simplistic, but they differ from the ancient Sumer and Akkad into the neo-Babylonian and Semitic tongues, not to mention deviations brought in by the Assyrians and Chaldeans, not to mention the losses encountered when Cuneiform became Sanskrit, Arabic and Hieroglyphics. Our emphasis here is firstly on the Akkad-Babylonian works and secondly on the Sumer of Eridu, Nippur, etc.

This codex is not one-to-one with all findings that you will have to decipher. This is because of the use of the language and the transliterations of the tablets. A word like LIKU, meaning "to receive", is found below. However, the Seeker will come across TALAKI and LIKIMA if they were to transcribe, for example, Anunnaki Prayers from the "*Grimoire of the Lifting of the Hand*". These other synonyms may not be found listed here because only their root is necessary to linguists – and it would be very costly and spacious to document each variation of a word, something people often take for granted in the English language ("receive", "received", "receiving", "receiver", etc.).[23]

---

23 See also *Liber-I* ('*Secrets of Sumerian Language*'), which contains the complete version of the Mardukite Chamberlains Cypher Manuscript along with illustrated cuneiform signs; or background story only found in the abridged *Liber-I* discourse portion in '*Truth Seeker's Guide to Cuneiform Writing*'.

TABLET SEEKERS LEXICON
(REVISED)

A - "on"
AB. - "father"
ABALU - "to bring away", "carry", "remove"
ABAN BIRKI - "thunderbolt"
ABARU - "strength", "to be strong"
ABBN - "serpent"
ABBUTTU - "chain", "fetter"
ABKALLU - "intermediate", "arbiter"
ABNU - "stone", can be prefix for type
ABRN - "nest"
AB.SIN - "constellation to INANNA-ISHTAR"
ABU - "father"
ABUBU - "deluge"
ABULL. - "city gate"
ABURRIS - "in security"
AB.ZU - "depths", "abyss", "south"
AD - "lame", "criple"
ADAD - "god of wind" or RAMMANU
ADAGURU - "incense-burner", "censer"
ADAKKN - "fever"
ADAPA - "wisest of men"
ADARU - "to fear"
ADDA-GUPPI - "high priestess of NANNA- SIN"
ADIRTU - "grief"
ADIRU - "trouble", "distress"
ADMU - "child"
AGA - "vessel", "clay pot", "cauldron"
AGAGU - "to be enraged"
AGGU - "angry"
AGUBBA - "water"
AHAMIS - "together"
AHAZU - "to hold", "to grasp"
AHHAZA - "robber spryte" {daemon}
AHU - "brother", "side"
AI - "not", "never"
AI - "god" ["ilu"]
AIABN - "sitting", "to sit"
AIBU - "foe"
AKALU - "to eat", "consume"
AKARU - "to be of value"
AKHKHARU - "vampyre"
A.KI.TI - "On-Earth, Life" [festival]
AL - "a digging tool", "a city"
ALA - "devil" {daemon}
ALADU - "to bear", "to beget"
ALAKTU - "path", "way"
ALAKU - "to go"
ALAL - "destroyer"

ALLALU - "bundle"
ALLA XUL - "evil god" {daemon}
ALTU - "wife"
ALU - "city", "daemon"
AMATU - "word", "speech"
AMILU - "man"
AMILUTU - "human-kind"
AMMINIM - "why?"
AN - "Heaven"
ANAKU - "I" [self]
ANA MINIM - "why?"
ANIHU – "faint", "tired"
ANNA - "sky", "heavens"
ANNI - "mercy"
ANNU - "sin"
ANNUM - "this"
ANNUMA. - "now", "herewith"
ANS(H)AR - "father of (the) heavens"
ANU(M) - "highest of the heavens"
ANU - "god" ["ilu"]
ANUNNA - "heavenly ones"
ANUNNAKI - "god" ["ilu"]
ANZU - "knower of Heaven"
APIN - "Mars" also LAHMU
APPARRATN - "headband"
APPARRITIN - "headband"
APSU - "god of sweet waters"
APIL - "son of", "offspring of"
APTU - "dwelling place", "habitation"
ARAD-KA - "servant," "worker"
ARAKU - "to lengthen", "long"
ARARU - "trembling", "to remble"
ARASU - "to meet"
ARBA - "a fortified city"
ARCHISM - "quickly"
ARDATU - "female" {maiden}
ARHU - "cow", "month"
ARINNN - "cloud"
ARKI - "behind"
ARKU - "green"
ARMAN - "smell", "scent"
ARN. - "sin", "crime", "punishment"
ARU - "to lead", "rule", "command law", "blossom"
AS - "spider", "wish", "curse"
ASABU - "to dwell", "to inhabit"
ASAMIN - "vessel"
ASAMINTNM - "tempest"
ASARIDU - "prince", "chief"
ASAR - "epithet of MARDUK"
ASARU - "to bless", "to be favorable towards"
ASASU - "to opress"
ASHARIDU - "eldest" [heir]
ASHR. - "place"
ASHSH - "because of", "concerning"
ASHSHAT - "wife"

ASPASTI - "marijuana"
ASRU - "place"
ASSUR - "god" ["ilu"]
ASSURA - "chamber" [specific]
ATALU - "eclipse"
ATFT - "to see"
ATMU - "speech", "word"
ATRA-HASIS - "the exceedingly wise"
ATRU - "abundant", "fat"
ATTA - "you", "thou"
AWAT. - "word"
AWIL. - "man"
AZAG - "god" ["ilu"] defeated by NINURTA

BA - "share", "pay", "omen"
BAU - "to share", "to come", "to bring"
BAALU - "to be mighty", "greatness"
BAALTU - "lady"
BA'ARU - "to hunt"
BAB(U) - "gate", "door", "ladder"
BABALU - "to bring", "supply"
BAGARUM - "to claim legally"
BAIIITU - "dried"
BALATU - "to live", "life", "living" [prosperous]
BALU - "without"
BAN - "to brighten"
BA'N - "to come"

BANI. "builder", "maker", "creator of"
BANITU - "brightness", "mercy"
BANU - "to build", "to create"
BINUTU - "creature", "creation" [offspring]
BARARU - "to howl"
BARRA - "depart", "begone" [forceful]
BARU - "to see", "perceive", "perception"
BASHUM - "to be"
BASU - "to have", "having", "to be", "being"
BEL - "god of the earth" [traditionally, ENLIL] also BIL
BEL. - "lord", "overlord" also BELU
BEL-MARDUK - "god of Babylon] also ASSUR
BELT. - "lady", "mistress" also BELITU
BENNA - "pestilence"
BERU - "a measurement" (one twelfth)
BIKITU - "to weep", "shedding tears"
BILIT - "god" ["ilu"]
BILU - "lord", "to rule"
BILTU - "lady"
BINU - "shrub-tree"

BIRIT UZNI - "understanding"
BIRKU - "knee"
BIRU - "vision"
BIRTU - "glance"
BISH. - "possession", "property"
BITU - "house"
BNANN - "muscle"
BUANU - "muscle"
BUKRU - "first-born"
BULLUTSUM - "to heal", "give life to"
BULU - "cattle"
BURASU - "cypress", "pine-wood" [incense]
BURZIGALLU - "a vessel"
BUTUKTU - "flood"
BUZUR - "solver of secrets", "serpent"

CHALAQUM - "to lose", "to be destroyed"
CHATT. - "staff", "scepter"
CHULLUQUM - "to destroy"
CHULQ - "lost object"

DABABUM - "to speak"
DADMU - "dwelling"
DADU - "love"
DAGAN - "god" ["ilu"]
DAIANU - "judge"
DAKU - "to slay"
DALAHU - "to disturb", "disorder", "chaos"
DALALU - "to bow down", "humbled"
DALHU - "disturbed", "confused" also
DALU - "to move"
DAMAKU - "being favorable"
DAMAMU - "weeping", "lament"
DAMKINA - "wife of EA-ENKI"
DAM.KI.NA - "lady-(t0)-Earth-came"
DANANU - "to be strong", "mighty"
DANNATU - "distress"
DANNUM - "strong", "powerful"
DANU - "to judge"
DAPARU - "to remove"
DARIS - "forever"
DARIUM - "everlasting"
DARU - "eternal" also DARUM
DARRU - "strong"
DASPU - "mead"
DISPU - "honey"
DIIPA - "honey"
DIKTU - "slaughter", "battle"
DILBAD - "a plant"
DIL.GAN - "Jupiter"
DINANU - "substitute"
DINGIR - "god", "mighty spirit power" ["ilu", "El"]
DINGIR XUL - "evil god" {daemon}
DINU - "judge", "judgment"

DIPARU - "torch"
DIR.GA - "dark chamber"
DISU - "abounding", "numerous"
DUB - "pincers", "tongues"
DULU - "hill"
DUMU.ZI - "son who is Life"
DUPPU - "tablet"
DUR.AN.KI - "bond-heaven-earth"
DURU - "wall", "fortress"
DUS - "a stone"
DUSUPU - "mead"

E. - "house", "abode", "residence"
EA - "god of the deep wisdom" [traditionally ENKI]
EDELU - "to shut"
E.DIN - "eden" - "home of the righteous ones"
EDIN NA ZU - "go waste in the desert"
EGIRM - "thought"
EISEPN - "owl"
EKALL. - "palace", "castle keep"
EKIMMN - "ghost" {ancestral ?}
E.KUR - "house which is like a mountain"
ELI - "on", "upon"
EL(I)T - "to go up"
ELISHU - "on it"
ELLUM - "pure", "holy"
ELU - "high", "highest", "of above"
ELUM - "to ascend", "to rise up"
EM - "meteorite"
EMEDU - "to stand"
EN - "master"
E.NINNU - "house (temple-shrine) of Fifty"
ENKI.DU - "Enki (has) created"
ENS(H)AG - "lofty lord" (half-earthling son of Marduk)
ENZU - "god of moon" [traditionally NANNA-SIN]
EPUUSH - "I made"
EQL. - "field"
EREBU - "to enter"
E.RI.DU - "house (in the) faraway, built"
ERINN - "cedar"
ERRA - "annihilator" (an epithet of NERGAL)
ERRESH. - "farmer", "tenant"
ERRET. - "curse", "malevolent speech"
ERTSET. - "planet land", "earth"
ESA - "to set"
E.SAG.IL - "house with lofty head", Temple to Marduk
ESENU - "to stink", "foul"

ETA - "dark", "to be darkness"
ETEQUM - "to pass"
ETSENT - "bone"
ETUTU - "gloom"
EZEN - "festival"
EZZUM - "angry"

FALLAHIN - "workers"

GA - "a plant"
GALALN - "enslaved"
GALATA - "to frighten"
GALLA - "devil" {daemon} also GALLU
GALTA - "terrible"
GALLUTU - "quaking"
GAMALU - "to complete", "maintain"
GAMRU - "perfect"
GARNA - "censer"
GASRU - "to be strong", "mighty"
GASSU - "plaster"
GELAL - "incubus"
GESNU - "alabaster" *abnu-gesnu*
GIBIL - "god of fire"
GIBILLA - "torch"
GIBSU - "mass", "volume"
GIGAB - "liquid offering", "libation"
GIGIM XUL - "evil spirit"
GILTANN - "water droplet"
GIMILL. - "favor"

GIMILLU - "a present", "gift"
GIMRU - "the whole", "totality"
GIPARU - "field"
GIRRA - "fires of the (sun-star) god"
GIRRN - "hinge"
GISH.BIL - "he who has fire" also GIBIL
GISPARRA - "snare"
GISSAKANA - "door"
GITMALU - "perfect"
GITMALUM - "a prefect", "a noble"
GUD.ANNA - "bull of heaven"
GUDDINN - "bat"
GUSURU - "wooden beam", "branch"
GU.UTU - "lamb of the sun" [Mercury(?)]
GUZI - "a vessel"

HADU - "rejoice", "joyful"
HATU - "to sin"
HALAKU - "to perish", "destroy"
HALALU - "to creep"
HALAPU - "to be dressed in"
HAM - "to scorch", "fry"
HAMSLTA - "to burn", "frying"
HARA - "ditch"
HARARU - "to dig", "plough"
HARASU - "to split", "dividing"
HARBA - "desolate"

HARBASTT - "rain"
HARBASU - "storm", "fury"
HAR-HAR - "a plant"
HARRU - "a wood"
HASBN - "pot"
HASBU - "pot"
HILU - "to tremble", "shake"
HIMITU - "butter"
HINZN - "mucus"
HIPU - "to wash"
HIMITU - "butter"
HITTU - "lintel", "sin"
HULUPPU - "tree" [willow?]
HUPPA - "bent"
HURASU - "gold"
HURSU - "mountain", "hill"
HUSSU - "ceremonial robe"

IA / I.A - "god" ["ilu"] ENKI
IAGASU - "to tear into pieces"
IAHAHU - "to waste"
IAHARRATA - "vessel"
IALAPU - "break out", "disperse"
IALASU - "triple"
IALATN - "to slit"
IAPASU - "to touch"
IARBAT(U)N - "to roam"
ID - "arm", "side"
IDDISSU - "newly shining"
IDIDN - "straight"
IDIRTU - "affliction"
IDIMMU - "daemon"
IDLU - "hero"
IDPA - "fever"
IDU - "hand", "side", "to know"
IDUM - "to know"
IFMN - "bone"
IG - "door"
IGIGI - "god" ["ilu"] "watchers (of the door/gate)"
IGIRU - "thought form"
IGU - "sin"
IHTAGGAAMUNE - "in my soreness" [affliction]
IHTUKAMUNE - "in my soreness" [affliction]
IIBBN - "serpent"
IIGNIIII - "a wood"
IKALLU - "palace"
IKIMMU - "spectre"
IKBU - "heel"
IKDU - "mighty", "courageous"
IKILU - "to be dark"
IKKARU – "husband"
IKLITU - "darkness"
IKRIBU - "prayer"
IKU - "needy"
IKUTU - "need", "want"
IKUNN - "to rob"
ILANI - "gods" pl.
ILTI - "spell", "charm"
ILTU - "straw"
ILU - "god" also IL. and ILAT.
IMA - "when", "in", "among"
IMIDU - "to stand", "establish"
IMMER. - "sheep"

IMMU - "day", "daylight"
IMNU - "right", "right side"
IMTU - "breath", "poison"
IN. - "eye" or plural INAN
INA - "in", "with", "from within", "among"
INNINNU - "corn"
INSU - "weak"
INU - "eye"
INUMA - "when" also ENUMA (e.g. Enuma Elis)
INUU - "to annul", "to alter", "invalidated"
IPIRU - "to support", "sustaining"
IPISU - "to do", "to make", "perform (a task)"
IPRU - "dust"
IRIBU - "to enter", "bring in", "flight of locusts"
IRRA - "plague-god", "famine" [NERGAL]
IRTU - "breast"
ISHAKKUS - "princess" [Lagash]
ISHAT. - "fire"
ISHD. - "foundation"
ISHTU - "from"
ISIPPNTU - "priestcraft"
ISIPU - "to add to", "increase"
IS(H)TAR - "goddess of love and war"
ISTU - "from"
ISU - "to have", "to be of"
ITIKU - "to remove", "tear away"
ITILLU - "mighty", "exalted"
ITIRU - "to protect"
ITPISU - "prudent"
ITS. - "tree", "wood"
ITTFT - "pitch"
ITTI - "with"
ITTN - "appearance"
IUTU - "form"
IXALASN - "to tear"
IZIBU - "to save", "deliver from"
IZIRU - "to trickle"
IZIZU - "to be angry"
IZZU - "mighty", "terrible"

KA - "a measure"
KABASU - "to spread"
KABATI - "heavy"
KABITTUM - "heavy / honored /important person"
KABLU - "battle", "waist of", "middle"
KABRU - "grave"
KABRXL - "grave"
KABSA - "fillet", "slay"
KABTU - "weighty", "important [person] also "kabtum"
KADADU - "to bow down"
KADIITU - "prostitute"
KADRUM - "wild", "fierce"
KAIAN - "continuously",

"constantly"
KAIANU - "continual", "constant"
KAKKABU - "star", "planet", "celestial body"
KAKKADU - "head"
KAKKU - "weapon"
KAL. - "totality", "entirety", "all parts"
KALAMU - "all", "of every sort"
KALU - "burning"
KALAPU - "to move"
KAMALU - "to be angry"
KAMANU - "cake"
KAMARUM - "to pile up", "to heap up"
KAMASU - "to bow", "to humble oneself"
KAMSBRU - "fall"
KANAKKU - "door gape"
KAN - "to guard", "guarding"
KANN - "base"
KANPA - "mark well", "remember", "conjure"
KANU - "to be firm", "to standfast", "reed"
KAPADA - "to begin"
KAPRA - "atonement"
KAPU - "to fall"
KARABU - "to be favorable", "to bless" also KARABUM
KARANU - "wine"
KARARA - "to turn"
KARD - "to bend"
KARDU - "brave", "valiant" also KARRADU
KARNANU - "horned"
KARU - "wall", "fortress-keep"
KASASU - "destroy"
KASAPU - "to pay rites of offering"
KASHSHAPTU - "wicked witch"
KASHAD - "to reach", "to arrive at"
KASITU - "bonds"
KASPU - "silver" (root KASP = silver)
KAS.SAG - "a liquid offering" [libation]
KASU - "to bind"
KATNU - "little"
KATRINNU - "smoke-offering"
KATU - "hand"
KDRA - "pain"
KHURATS - "gold" (e.g. carats)
KI - "seat of life", "gate of gods"
KIA - "earth"
KI.AM - "thus", "as follows"
KIBITU - "word", "command"
KIBRATU - "region", "zonei", "quarter of Heaven"
KIGAL - "great below"

KIISARRA - "bandage"
KILATE - "both"
KILALLI - "both"
KILLATU - "sin", "disgrace"
KIMA - "as", "like", "that", "when"
KIMD - "flour"
KIMTU - "family"
KIMU - "grain"
KINAZN - "halter"
KINGU - "husband of TIAMAT"
KINIS - "truly"
KINNU - "nest"
KINZA - "flat"
KINU - "sure", "certain", "true"
KIPA - "to bend"
KIPPATA - "twig", "end", "corner"
KIR. (KIRI.) - "orchard", "garden of fruit"
KIRBU - "in the midst"
KIRU - "pitch"
KISADU - "neck"
KIS(H)AR - "father of the earth"
KISPU - "magick", "enchantment", "spell"
KISRU - "might", "strength"
KISSARN - "width"
KISSATU - "the whole", "a host of many", "legions"
KISU IN KIS LIBBI - "pain of the heart"
KITTU - "truth", "righteousness"
KU - "cord", "barley"
KU.A.TIR - "grain"
KU.BABBAR - "silver"
KUDURRU - "boundary stone", "landmark"
KUGI - "bright from the earth", "gold"
KULA - "snare", "net"
KULIPTU - "scales"
KULTU - "canopy"
KULU - "voice"
KU.MAL - "the Ram", "field-dweller" ("Aries")
KUMARU - "armlet"
KUMMO - "yours", "thine", "thy"
KUNUKKU - "seal", "cylinder seal"
KUPPU - "wellsprings", "source"
KUR - "land" [esp. mountain]
KURGAL - "great land" [Sumer]
KURKUR (sammu) - "a plant"
KURMATU - "food"
KURU - "in need", "distress"
KUSAS - "destruction"

LA - "not"
LA'ABU - "to oppress"
LAAHN - "teeth gum"
LAATA - "cow"
LABANU - "to cast down"
LABASHUM - "to put on", "to

wear"
LABASU - "ghoul" {daemon} also "to clothe oneself"
LABARTU - "hag-daemon"
LABIRUM - "old"
LABUTTU - "chief"
LAHMU - "monster", also "Mars"
LA(K)HMU - "serpent god"
LA(K)HAMU – "mosiure goddess" consort of the above
LALARTU - "phantom", "wailing", "crying aloud"
LALASSU - "spectre"
LAMA - "before"
LAMADU - "to learn", "to teach" also LILMADU
LAMASSU - "guardian spirit"
LANN - "shape"
LAPATU - "to surround", "to touch" also LAPAT-UM
LARU - "shoots", "buds"
LIARU - "tree"
LIBBU - "heart", "center" (root is LIBB.)
LIBITTU - "brick" (root is "LIBITT.")
LIKU - "to receive", "to take"
LILA - "phantom spirit"
LILITU - "female phantom spirit" {daemon}
LIM. - "thousand"
LIMNU - "evil"
LISANU - "tongue"
LITU - "strength", "headband"
LI'U - "strong", "strength", "tablet"
LU - "or", "either" (e.g. LU... LU... "either.. or..")
LU - "man", "secretion of", etc.
LUATI - "unclean"
LUBLUBU - "trap"
LU.GAL - "king", lit. "great man"
LU.LU - "the mixed one" [hybrid humans]
LUMNU - "evil"

MACHARUM - "to face", "to encounter"
MACHR. - "front"
MA'DU - "many"
MADUTU - "great quantity"
MAGAN - "Egypt", "dark lands"
MAGARU - "listening intently", "receive a friend"
MAGARUM - "to agree to"
MA.GUR.GUR – "submersible boat"
MAHRU - "before"
MAIADA - "to bring low"
MAIU - "to forget"
MAKAL - "food"
MAKALU - "eating"

MAKATU - "to fall"
MAKHATSUM - "to beat", "to strike"
MALA - "as many as"
MALIKU - "prince", "counselor"
MALIUTI - "to cry over"
MALU - "to fill", "to be filled", "full"
MAMIT - "ban", "tapu" [taboo, restriction]
MAMITU - "ban", "curse"
MAMLU - "strong"
MAMMA - "whosoever", "whatsoever"
MANNU - "who" also MANNUM
MANU - "to repeat", "recite"
MANZAZU - "station", "a place"
MAQATUM - "to fall"
MARDUK - "god" ["ilu"]
MARKITI - "to mash up", "pulverize"
MARSU - "sick" also MARTSUM, MARUSHTUM
MARTU - "daughter" (root is MART.)
MARU - "son" (root is MAR.)
MARUSTU - "pain", "misfortune", "disaster"
MASH.TAB.BA - "twins" [e.g. Gemini]
MASKIM XUL - "evil fiend"
MASLA - "middle"
MAS.MASU - "priest"
MASS - "guide"
MASSLTA - "to humble", "humbled"
MASSU - "ruler"
MASTAKAL - "a plant"
MASTI - "broadness", "be broad", "oil anointing"
MASU - "to forget"
MATU - "land" (root is MAT.)
MA'U - "water" also MU
MAZALTA - "home"
ME - "divine formulae", "tablets of destiny"
MELUHHA - "black mountain"
MERESHT - "cultivation" ["field"]
MESTAKAL - "a plant"
MILKU - "counsel"
MILN - "strength" [full power]
MIMMA SUMSU - "anything", "of whatever kind"
MINUM - "what?"
MINUTU - "incantation", "repetitive recitation"
MISARU - "righteousness", "justice" (root is MISHAR.)
MISRU - "property", "wealth"

MITTH - "rain"
MITU - "dead"
MU - "water", "name"
MUDISSU - "renewer", "renovator"
MUDU - "understanding", "wise"
MUL - "star", "planet", "celestial body"
MULLA XUL - "evil devil"
MULU-GISGAL-LU - "a plant"
MUMMU - "god" ["ilu"], [Mercury(?)]
MU.MU - "a priest"
MUSGARRU - "a stone"
MUSU - "night" also MUSH.

NABATU - "to shine"
NABNITU - "creation"
NABU - "who speaks for" [prophet son of MARDUK]
NA'BU - "to name" - SUMMA
NABU "to exist", "be"
NADANUM - "to give"
NADARA - "to rage"
NADU - "exalted", "praised" - "to cast", "to place"
NADUM - "to throw"
NAGASUM - "to please", "to agree with"
NAGIRU - "patron"
NAHASU - "to abound in", "abundance" - NUHSU
NAKARA - "destroy"
NAKARU - "to rebel", "be hostile", "alter", "be altered"
NAKASU - "to cut off", "to cut down" (NAKASUM)
NAKD - "libation"
NALAKU - "to bite"
NAM - "to attack" [smite]
NAMARU - "to shine", "to be bright" - NAMRU
NAMKUR. - "possession"
NAMMASSU - "reptile", "lizard-creature"
NAMRASIT - "god" ["ilu"]
NAMTARU - "pestilence"
NANNAR - "the bright one"
NANNARU - "god of moon" [NANNA-SIN]
NAPASU - "to lay low"
NAPISTU - "life"
NAPSASTU - "ointment"
NARABU - "to break"
NARAM - "to help"
NARBU - "greatness", "might" also NIRBU
NARU - "stream"
NASAHU - "to remove", "tear away"
NASARU - "to bring low", "to keep", "preserve"
NASKU - "weak"
NASSIKA - "to put", "place"
NATALU - "to see", "behold"
NATFUIA - "parting gift" [rare final good-bye]

NATSARUM - "to guard", "to keep safe"
NAZAKU - "to destroy"
NAZAZU - "to stand"
NEBO - "messenger god" also NABU
NE.IBRU - "Nippur"
NERGAL - "god of the underworld", "death-god"
NHUL(U)N - "alkali"
NIBRU.KI - "crossing-navel of the Earth"
NIDATA - "desolate place"
NIDITT - "gift"
NIGISSN - "cavern"
NIK - "to slay"
NIKU - "to offer"
NIN.A.GAL - "prince of great waters" son of ENKI
NINDABU - "offering"
NINGAL - "god" ["ilu"], "great lady"
NINGISHZIDA - "prince-lord-tree-life"
NINLIL - "wife of ENLIL"
NIRGAL - "god" ["ilu"] also NERGAL
NISABA - "god" ["ilu"] "goddess of writing"
NISH. - "oath", "life pledge"
NISHU - "people"
NISU - "to remove", "tear away", "be removed"
NISU - "to raise", "to lift"
[prayer, necromantics"
NISUTU - "male relatives"
NI'U - "turn", "restrain"
NIULT(U)N - "vein"
NMAII(U)N - "disease" [affliction]
NPA - "cloud"
NPIIU - "enchantment"
NPP(U)N - "cloudy"
NRBAT(U)N - "reed bush", "willow tree"
NSUMGALLUIII - "dragon"
NSUZZU - "standing"
NTLN - "embrace"
NTUKK(U)N - "spirit"
NTUTU - "chosen"
NUBATU - "to shine"
NUBATTU - "a festival"
NUKHSH. - "abundance"
NURU - "light"
NUSKU - "fire-god"

PA.BIL - "god's defender", "the Archer" [Sagittarius]
PADU - "to set free", "to spare one"
PAGRU - "body", "corpse"
PAIN - "axe"
PAITU - "flax"
PAKADU - "to take care of", "to rule", "to entrust"
PALAHU - "to fear", "to terrify", "to rever-

ence"
PALAKHUM – see PALAHU
PAN. - "front", "face" (plural)
PANU - "face"
PAPANN - "navel"
PAQADUM - "to care for"
PARAKKU - "shrine"
PARAKU - "to block up"
PARAN - "to cut off", "separate"
PARASU - "to decide", "to separate into parts", "cut"
PARIITU - "wise woman"
PARUTU - "alabaster"
PARSU - "command"
PASAHU - "to be consoled", "pacified"
PASASU - "to rub", "to anoint"
PASATU - "a brightly colored robe"
PASHATUM - "to erase"
PASSURU - "dish", "vessel" [ointments]
PATARU - "to tear", "to loosen", "to remove"
PATINNN - "girdle"
PAZRN - "secret"
PETSUM - "white"
PETU - "open"
PIRU - "young", "offspring"
PITIKTII - "mud wall"
PITU - "to open" - PETU
PNRIDN - "therefore"
PNRIMN - "wild ass"

PU - "mouth" also PUM
PUHRU - "totality", "the whole"
PUKKU - "drum"
PUKLN - "tow"
PULANU - "such and such"
PULUCHT. - "fear"
PULUHTU - "terror"
PURSITN - "separated"
PURSUMTU - "old woman"
PURUSS. - "decision"
PUSHQ. "difficulty"
PUSKN - "misery", "sorrow" also PUSKU

QABUM - "to say"
QAT. - "hand"
QIST. - "present", "gift"

RABISU - "daemon"
RABUM - "a great" also RABITUM
RAGAMUM - "to raise a legal claim"
RAKASU - "to bind", "to knot"
RAMMANU - "god of wind" also ADAD
RAMMU - "to shriek"
RAMU - "love"
RAPASU - "to be broad", "broadness" (RAPASHUM)
RASBU - "mighty", "powerful"

RASI - "to possess", "to grant" - also ARSI
RE (R'I) - "shepherd"
RIDD - "to seize", "hold back"
RIHA - "spawn" or "to spawn", "spawning"
RIHITU - "dregs"
RIHUTU - "spawning"
RIKSU - "band", "cord"
RIKU - "distanced", "to be distant"
RIKUTU - "distance"
RIM. - "beloved", "wild bull"
RIMKU - "libation"
RIMNU - "merciful"
RIMU - "mercy"
RISATI - "shouts of joy"
RISHAN - "top", "head"
RISU - "head", "to shout joyfully"
RISTU - "former", "original", "preeminent"
RITA - "to set", "setting" [...in place]
RITTU - "hand", "fist", "wrist" (root is RITT.)
RITU - "pasture"
RNH - "witchcraft"
RUB. - "prince", "noble"
RUBATU - "princess"
RUBU - "prince"
RUBUINTU - "marsh"
RUHU - "sorcery", "enchantment"
RUKU - "distant"
RUSA - "sorcery" also RUSU, RUSI
RUSSU - "skin"

SA - "who", "which" [religious pronoun]
SA - "a measure"
SAADU - "hunting", "to hunt"
SABARU - "chirping", "to break up"
SABASU - "to be angry"
SABATU - "to smite", "to grasp", "to seize"
SABU - "to bale up"
SADAHU - "to move along", "to advance"
SADU - "mountain"
SAHARU - "to turn towards"
SAHFLPA - "spreading", "to spread over"
SAHFUITL - "to fill"
SAHPNTOM - "widespreading"
SAHTURRA - "little pig"
SAGAMU - "to howl"
SAGGANAKKU - "a governor", "high official"
SAGKI - "temple-shrine"
SAHALU - "to summon", "draw forth"
SAHARRN - "pot"
SAKANU - "to set", "to place", "to establish", "be placed"

SAKAPU - "to cast down", "to overthrow"
SAKU - "to be high", "heights", "to be exalted"
SALA - "to sink", "sinking"
SALAHU - "to sprinkle"
SALAMU - "to be intact", "complete"
SALATU - "female relatives"
SALUMMATU - "light"
SALBABU - "mighty", "courageous"
SALMU - "darkness", "dark", "image", "intact"
SALU - "cough"
SAM - "to putrefy"
SAMAHU - "strong of heart"
SAMANN - "poison"
SAMARU - "to revere", "to worship"
SAMAS - "god" ["ilu"] also SHAMMASH or UTU
SAMMU KUR-KUR - "a plant"
SAMNU - "oil"
SAMRU - "violent"
SAMU - "to settle down", "establish outright", "heaven"
SA.NA - "vessel for incense", "censer"
SANANU - "to oppose", "to rival"
SANAQUM - "to come close"
SANFLKA - "to reach"
SAP - "gather" [esp. people]
SAPARU - "net", "to send"
SAPAK(U)N - "to pour out"
SAPCHUM - "scattered"
SAPLU - "that which is beneath", "behind", "under"
SAPPARU - "goat"
SAPSLNTI - "covered", "to cover"
SAP(U)N - "perishing", "to dissolve"
SARAHU - "to be bright"
SARAKU - "to sprinkle", "to pour out", "to offer"
SARHU - "powerful"
SARIRA - "a metal"
SARRU - "king"
SARRUM - "false", "lying"
SARN - "to pour"
SARU - "to weaken", "wind", "breeze"
SARURU - "splendor"
SASU - "he", "him", "they", "them" also SU
SASU - "to speak to the word of command", "invoke"
SATARU - "to write", "inscribe"
SATU - "to drink"
SEDU - "genius", "spirit"
SERT(U)N - "wickedness"
SHA. - "who", "whom", "which"
SHADALUM - "to be wide"

SHAKANUM - "to put", "to place", "to set"
SHAKN. - "governor"
SHALEM - "complete", epithet for SAMAS
SHALSH - "three"
SHALUM - "to ask", "inquire"
SHALUSHT - "one-third"
SHAMM. (SAM) - "plant"
SHAMN. - "plant oil"
SHAMU - "sky", "heavens"
SHANUM - "second", "other one"
SHAPARUM - "to send" (a message)
SHAQALUM - "to weigh out", "to play out"
SHAR - "king" also SHARR. or SHAR. "wind"
SHARA - "prince"
SHARAKUM - "to present to", "to give to"
SHARAQ - "thief"
SHARAQUM - "to steal"
SHARRAT. - "queen"
SHARRUT. - "kingship"
SHASUM - "to cry"
SHATARUM - "to write"
SHATT. - "year"
SHE. - "barley"
SHEBERUM - "to break"
SHEPAN - "feet"
SHIKAR - "beer"
SHINN - "tooth"
SHIPR. - "work"
SHIZB. - "milk"
SHU / SHUATI / SHIATI etc. - "that"
SHUBT - "seat", "dwelling"
SHUKLULUM - "to perfect", "to complete"
SHULM. - "wholeness", "health"
SHUM - "name", "offspring", "child of"
SHUMLU - "to fill"
SHUMMA - "if"
SHUNUTI - "those"
SHUQURUM - "very costly", "precious"
SHURSHUDUM - "to firmly found" or "plant"
SIBA - "seven"
SIBITTU - "imprisonment"
SIBRU - "wood"
SIBU - "old man"
SIDU - "guardian spirit"
SIGARU - "bolt"
SIHRU - "small"
SIHU - "high", "lofty"
SIKARU - "drink"
SIKKU - "mouse"
SIKKURN - "bolt"
SILAN - "setting"
SILN - "side"
SIMAN - "a plant"
SIMTU - "destiny"
SIMU - "to hear", "obedient",
S(U)IN - "god of moon"
SINNISHT. - "woman" (fem.)

SIPTU - "incantation"
SIPU - "foot"
SIPU - "to beseech" also SUPU
SIRGARRU - "a stone"
SIRTU - "iniquity"
SIRU - "mighty", "field", "flesh"
SI.SI - "a plant"
SISIT - "fingers"
SITTU - "misery"
SI'U - "to look", "to seek", "looking for"
SUBATU - "garment"
SUD - "one who nurses"
SU.EN - "end of incantation"
SUHUR.MASH - "goat-fish" [Capricorn]
SUKKALLU - "messenger"
SULIBU - "fox"
SULUL - "daemon"
SUMU - "garlic", "name"
SURBU - "powerful", "mighty"
SURMINU - "cypress"
SUTTU - "dream"

TABALN - "carry off"
TABANNU - "handiwork"
TABU - "to be good", "acceptable"
TAHTU - "victory"
TAIILTU - "joy"
TAMAHA - "to hold" also TAMAHU
TAMCHAR - "battle"
TAMKAR - "merchant"
TAMTU - "ocean"
TAMU - "to speak", "to declare"
TANIH(T)U - "sighing", "groaning"
TAPPINNU - "dough"
TAPPU - "helper"
TARADU - "to expel", "to send away"
TARAKA - "to burst"
TARLREN - "to straighten"
TARRINNU - "a sacrificial feast"
TARSIR - "a plant"
TARU - "to turn", "to return"
TASILTU - "decision"
TASLITU - "prayer"
TASMITU - "god" ["ilu"]
TEBITU - "submersible boat"
TELAL - "wicked warrior" {daemon}
TEM. - "news", "report", "information", "decision"
TEMEN - "foundation", "house" [temple]
TEMENOS - "wall" [temple]
TEMU - "understanding", "knowledge"
TERT. - "command", "omen"
TESU - "destroyer"
TI - "life", "rib"
TIBU - "to come"
TIHU - "to approach"

TIKU - "waist"
TIN-TIR - "Babylon"
TIM - "weave"
TIRHU - "oracle reader"
TIRTU - "soul", "spirit"
TITT. - "clay", also TITU
TI'U - "headache"
TIZKARU - "loud"
TSECHRUM - "small"
TSABATUM - "to seize"
TSALMUM - "black"
TSIBT / TSBT - "property", "farmland" (agriculture)
TSIRUM - "exalted"
TSUBAT. - "mantle", "garment", "vestment"
TU - "a plant"
TULTU - "worm"
TUMRU - "ashes"
TUPP. - "clay tablet"
TUPSARRU - "scribe" "tablet keeper"

U - "and", "to"
UB - "regions", "four cardinal directions"
UD - "weather", "sunlight", "storm"
UG - "lion", "dead", "to die"
UGARU - "plain, country"
UGGAE - "death-god"
UGGATU - "anger"
UKLU - "darkness"
UKNU - "lapis lazuli" also
UKURU - "plant"
UL - "not", "joy", "contentment"
ULTU - "from"
ULINN - "cord"
ULINNU - "robe", "vestment"
ULLUM - "that"
ULSU - "joy"
UMU - "storm", "day" (root is UM)
UMM - "mother"
UMMA - "thus" [spoken]
UNKATI - "rings"
UPU - "clouds"
URIS(U)N - "kid" {child}
URRU - "light"
URT(U)N - "explanation"
URU.DU - "copper"
URUKU - "larvae"
US - "foundation"
UTUK XUL - "evil spirit" {daemon}
UZNU - "ear" (root is UZN)
UZZU - "anger"

WALADUM - "to give birth to", "to bear"
WARD - "slave"
WARKI - "after"
WARQUM - "green" or "yellow-green" [color]
WASHABUM - "to sit", "to dwell"
WASHTUM - "difficult", "hard", "fierce"

WATAR - "excessive", "further driven", "determined"
YAU - "where" [question]
YASI - "me" also YATI
ZABAR - "bronze", "gleaming double metal"
ZAG - "flesh"
ZAIARU - "foe"
ZAKAPU - "to erect", "impale"
ZAKARU - "to name", "speak the command"
ZALIPTU - "wickedness"
ZAMA(U)N(U)N - "enemy"
ZANANU - "to rain", "raining"
ZARABU - "to restrain"
ZARPANITU – wife of MARDUK – also spelled with an "S"
ZER. - "seed"
ZI - "spirit"
ZI.BA.ANNA - "scales of fate", "life-decision-in heaven"
ZIKAR / ZIKR - "male", "man" (masc.)
ZIMU - "appearance"
ZINU - "to be angry"
ZIRU - "seed"
ZIRUTU - "hate"
ZITT. "share of", "portion of", "property of"
ZU - "legendary bird"
ZU.AB - "bright from the deep", "gold"
ZUMRU - "body"

**MARDUKITE
CHAMBERLAINS**

Would you like to know more???

**ENTER THE REALM
OF THE**

**MARDUKITE
CHAMBERLAINS**

The contents of this book were first pubished in 2009
as part of an esoteric occult underground serial.

The 2012 Mardukite Core Nostalgia Editions
by Joshua Free

NECRONOMICON : The Babylonian Grimoire (Liber-N – Lapis Edition)
NECRONOMICON LITURGY & LORE (Liber-L – Ruby Edition)
NECRONOMICON GATEKEEPERS GRIMOIRE (Liber- G – Emerald Edition)
NINE GATES OF THE KINGDOM OF SHADOWS (Liber-9 – Amethyst Edition)

For the complete version of this current series,
please refer to the Year-1 composite Liber-N+L+G+9 anthology
Necronomicon Anunnaki Bible by Joshua Free
now available in the revised and espanded 2012 Fifth Edition.

NECRONOMICON ANUNNAKI BIBLE
Edited by Joshua Free

The Necronomicon – a masterpiece of Mesopotamian Magick, Mysticism and primordial spirituality!

A Complete Necronomicon!

This definitive edition contains the complete Year 1 tablet cycle from the "Mardukite Chamberlains" including Liber N – **Necronomicon**, Liber LL – *Liturgy & Lore*, Liber GG – *Gatekeepers Grimoire* and the coveted Liber 9. These are the raw underground materials have shaped the existence of man's beliefs and practices for thousands of years – right from the heart of Sumer, Babylon and Egypt! A Mardukite compendium of intensive historical, spiritual and mystical research drawn from very real and researchable tablets... enough to support a very real "*Necronomicon*" Anunnaki revival tradition!

Join hundreds of others who have enjoyed the best of what the next generation has to offer. What has come before is but a shadow to the realizations now capable to all self-honest Truth Seekers! Rediscover the most ancient records of magick and mysticism – the most ancient traditions of Gods and Men lay here waiting to be unveiled!

GATES OF THE NECRONOMICON
Edited by Joshua Free

The complete Year 2 Liber 50+51+R anthology of the Mardukites with "Sumerian Religion", "Babylonian Myth & Magic" and "Necronomicon Revelations."

"Sumerian Religion" (Liber-50) will take you on a unique progressive journey that is just as relevant and critical today as it was thousands of years ago.

"Babylonian Myth & Magic" (Liber 51) is unparalleled in displaying the post-Sumerian mystery tradition of the ancient Babylonians. Discover how Babylon rose to the heights of its power from seemingly prehistoric nothingness and how these systems are still with us!

"Necronomicon Revelations" (Liber R) illustrates how spiritual beings have influenced the imaginations of 'metaphysical' artists and writers, increasingly during the last century. Discover the forces that are behind all of the systems installed in human consciousness, both 'social' and 'mystical', since the time of the ancient Sumerian Anunnaki.

THE BOOK OF ELVEN-FAERIE
by Joshua Free

The original underground masterpiece *comes alive* and in print available to the public for the *first time ever!* Follow the ancient traditions of Mesopotamia as they evolve into the systems of Western Europe.

Discover how the most arcane practices actually shaped the beliefs of the western world and learn how mystical lineages of modern "folk magic" can be actually traced through the evolution of human civilization on the planet – all the way back to the ancient Anunnaki traditions of Sumerians, Babylonians, Egyptians, etc. and becoming the practices of the Tuatha de Dannan (Tuatha d'Anu) and other Celtic tribes.

Ever popular in the underground, this book includes the complete *Book of Elven-Faerie* discourse with its corresponding "Grimoires" of Elven-Faerie traditions and forest magick, bring a complete Elvish Tradition to light for the first time in printed history. This book restores the historical basis of the modern "New Age" move-ments resulting from one Seeker's pursuits into the origins of the "Druids."

THE BOOK OF MARDUK
by Joshua Free

The original Anunnaki devotional companion of the modern revival returns in an oversized full-color deluxe ceremonial edition!

The Book of Marduk (by Nabu) is a long-lost out-of-print 'tablet collection' that paved the way for intensive research and experi-mentation using Joshua Free's '*Necronomicon Anunnaki Bible*' and essentially comprises the internal methods of the 'Order of Nabu' to acquire communication and establish a relationship with 'alien intelligences' via a program of ancient-styled Babylonian-inspired 'Mardukite' initiation, dedication and devotion; reviving the same process used by ancient priests of the Sumerian Anunnaki in Mesopotamia.

Original never-before-seen 'incantation-prayers' appear in both English and Akkadian/Babylonian.

The 'Book of Marduk' composes *Liber-W* and the Tablet-W series of the revised and expanded fifth edition of the '*Necronomicon Anunnaki Bible*' edited by Joshua Free.

ABOUT THE AUTHOR
JOSHUA FREE

Known as "Merlyn Stone" in the 1990's, **Joshua Free** reappeared on the scene in 2008 with the launch of *Mardukite Ministries* on the Summer Solstice that year.

He is the *Archbishop-Patesi* of the *Mardukite Archdiocese of North America* and the *Mardukite Chamberlains, Nabu Maerdechai*. Joshua is also the founder of the *NexGen Systemology Society*.

His prolific writings include: *Arcanum, Book of Elven-Faerie, Sumerian Religion, Necronomicon Anunnaki Bible,* and *The Sorcerer's Handbook of Merlyn Stone* among several others.

In 2011 he released his first published work of fiction titled *The Hybrids*.

Printed in Poland
by Amazon Fulfillment
Poland Sp. z o.o., Wrocław